Kaitlyn M

111 Places
in Montreal
That You Must
Not Miss

Photographs by Bethany Livingstone

emons:

To my guardian angels, my Nanny Shirley and Nanny Emma

Bibliographical information of the Deutsche Nationalbibliothek
The Deutsche Nationalbibliothek lists this publication in
the Deutsche Nationalbibliografie; detailed bibliographical data
are available on the internet at http://dnb.d-nb.de.

© Emons Verlag GmbH
All rights reserved
© Photographs by Bethany Livingstone, except see page 238
© Cover icon: pngaaa.com-3044913
Layout: Eva Kraskes, based on a design
by Lübbeke | Naumann | Thoben
Maps: altancicek.design, www.altancicek.de
Basic cartographical information from Openstreetmap,
© OpenStreetMap-Mitwirkende, OdbL
Edited by: Karen E. Seiger
Printing and binding: Grafisches Centrum Cuno, Calbe
Printed in Germany 2024
ISBN 978-3-7408-1721-3
First edition

Guidebooks for Locals & Experienced Travelers
Join us in uncovering new places around the world at
www.111places.com

Foreword

I moved to Montreal the day after my high school graduation. I had known from the first time I set foot in the city during a junior high school trip that it was where I was meant to grow into myself. The bright lights, the good food and wine, the *joie de vivre* … there's no city in North America quite like it.

I've spent the entire decade of my twenties – and then some – navigating the city, and I will never stop waxing poetic about how special and unique Montreal is. The old-world charm and ever-so-slight pretentiousness of this place (sorry) juxtaposed with the grunge and electric creativity that pulse within the city limits offers a natural sophistication and well-roundedness akin to a chic European city. But the affordable nature and social services available in Montreal and Quebec as a whole also mean that young people can afford to live a full life here without fear of being forced to move elsewhere.

Montreal is truly a patchwork of artists, creatives, and *bon vivants,* all swirling together to create something vibrant and decadent. There is no other place in Canada where I'd rather live. This book is a passionate love letter and tribute to the city that raised me. I wanted to create this book for both lifelong and newly minted Montrealers alike. It's a companion to take with you on weekend walks with friends all through the city to search for hidden treasures, or on family strolls to find the secret stories around your own neighbourhood.

From *plein air* sculpture gardens and a quirky penguin colony to world-class libraries and shimmering cabarets, this collection of 111 places was designed to surprise, enlighten, and inspire, and I can't wait for you to start checking them off your list. Consider this your own personal invitation to fall in love with Montreal the way I did – over and over again.

111 Places

1___ Acro Park Studio
Where clowning around is a requirement | 10

2___ Allan Memorial Institute
Dark history hidden in plain sight | 12

3___ Alley Cat Gallery
A cat-focused public art institution | 14

4___ Atrium Le 1000
Go skating in a skyscraper | 16

5___ Auberge du Dragon Rouge
Drink your way to medieval times | 18

6___ Auberge Saint Gabriel
Share a round of Shirley Temples with a ghost | 20

7___ Bain Morgan
Beaux Art bathhouse | 22

8___ The Barbie Expo
The world's largest Barbie doll exhibition | 24

9___ Bed-In for Peace
John & Yoko slept here | 26

10___ Berlin Wall Segment
Poetic spot for a heavy piece of history | 28

11___ Bison Bust at Joe Beef
An unsuspected bathroom attendant | 30

12___ Cabaret Lion d'Or
Century-old entertainment | 32

13___ Cabaret Mado
Sparkle at this gender-bending institution | 34

14___ Camillien-Houde Lookout
Panoramic views and paranormal activity | 36

15___ Canada Malting Co.
Urban exploration on the banks of the Lachine Canal | 38

16___ CCA Garden
Public art and plenty of people-watching | 40

17___ Centre Toussaint
Cooking, Creole, and Haitian history | 42

18___ Céramic Café Studio
Colour me happy | 44

19___ Cheap Thrills Records
The wonky purple stairway to music heaven | 46

20___ Cinema L'Amour
A safe space to get your juices flowing | 48

21___ Comedy Nest
Get your laugh on – for less | 50

22___ Copernicus Monument
An ode to the Polish astronomer and mathematician | 52

23___ Crew Collective & Café
Become the main character | 54

24___ The Daniel McAllister Tug
Visit the largest preserved tugboat in Canada | 56

25___ Dora Wasserman Theatre
One of the last Yiddish theatres in the world | 58

26___ Dorchester Square
Picnic atop a former gravesite | 60

27___ Dragon Flowers
The flower queen of the Mile End | 62

28___ Ecomuseum Zoo
Owls and foxes and bears – oh my! | 64

29___ Emergence of the Chief
A striking dedication to the Kanien'kehá:ka people | 66

30___ Eva B. Boutique
Saint Laurent's best treasure trove | 68

31___ Fireworks Festival
The best seat in the house is a folding chair | 70

32___ First Nations Garden
Indigenous culture from the ground up | 72

33___ Fleming Mill
The only Anglo-Saxon mill in Quebec | 74

34___ Geordie Theatre & School
The city's leading English-language theatre | 76

35___ Gibbys Restaurant
Dining in a 200-year-old stable | 78

36___ Gibeau Orange Julep Cruise Night
Hot rods and hotdogs | 80

37___ The Gorgosaurus Skeleton
Who knew a dinosaur went to McGill? | 82

38___ Grey Nuns Residence Crypt
Resting inside and beneath the Motherhouse | 84

39 Guimard Metro Entrance
Take an afternoon trip to Paris – by public transit | 86

40 Habitat 67
Brutalist brilliance | 88

41 Haunted McTavish Monument
A moneyed mystery | 90

42 The Heart from Auschwitz
Through the eyes of Montreal's survivors | 92

43 Henri Henri Hats
The birth of the hat trick | 94

44 Holiday Inn Koi Pond
Wind down in Chinatown | 96

45 Indigenous Voices of Today
A powerful display of resilience | 98

46 Jacques de Lesseps Park
It's a bird! It's a plane! | 100

47 Jeanne Mance Monument
The founding mother of Montreal medicine | 102

48 John McCaffery's Grave
A not-so-touching tombstone | 104

49 Largest Wooden Coaster
Soar through the air with the greatest of anxiety | 106

50 La Boutique Boreale
Thoughtful souvenirs | 108

51 La Sala Rossa
Vamos a bailar | 110

52 Le HonkyTonk de Lachine
Learn to line dance | 112

53 Leonard Cohen Home
Where the music lived | 114

54 Liberté Commemorative Monument
What went down during the October Crisis | 116

55 Louverture Monument
A Haitian hero | 118

56 Maison Antoine-Beaudry
Where historic architecture meets contemporary art | 120

57 Marché aux Puces Métropolitain
Hot commodity of oddities | 122

58 Marché Ghanacan
A pillar of the Ghanaian community | 124

59 — Marché Maisonneuve
The little public market that could | 126

60 — Maude Abbott Medical Museum
A museum with a warning label | 128

61 — Ministry of Cricket
Gym class, all grown up | 130

62 — Minuit Dix Tattoo Shop
A queer-owned ink institution | 132

63 — Montreal Aviation Museum
Look up! | 134

64 — Montreal Insectarium
Pretty in pink | 136

65 — Montreal Irish Memorial
The world's oldest Irish Famine memorial | 138

66 — Montreal Signs Project
Illuminating local heritage | 140

67 — Montreal Stock Exchange
Buy low, sell high | 142

68 — Montreal's Birthplace
The origins of a metropolis | 144

69 — Mordecai Richler's Residence
The pearl of the Golden Square Mile | 146

70 — Morgan Arboretum
Go forest bathing | 148

71 — Musée des Ondes Emile Berliner
The history of electromagnetic waves | 150

72 — Mussolini Fresco
The only church to feature the dictator | 152

73 — National Archives in Montreal
A stunning beaux arts bibliothèque | 154

74 — NHL Centre Ice
A piece of Habs history | 156

75 — Norman Bethune Square
A Canadian hero in China | 158

76 — Notre Dame Basilica
Walk down the aisle where Celine Dion tied the knot | 160

77 — Nouilles de Lan Zhou
Freshness is the name of the game | 162

78 — N Sur MacKay
Where everybody knows your name | 164

79___ Old Port Fishing
Get hooked on downtown fishing | 166

80___ Oscar Peterson Mural
An homage to the late king of Canadian jazz | 168

81___ Pang Pang Karaoke
A night of karaoke – without the stage fright | 170

82___ Parc Ahuntsic
Universally accessible fun for all | 172

83___ Parc Jeanne Mance
A park for all with land-locked beach volleyball | 174

84___ The Peace Treaty of 1701
The alleged end to a century of hostility | 176

85___ Penguins in the Plateau
Peep the penguins in the window | 178

86___ Place Marie-Josèphe Angélique
The immortal face of liberation | 180

87___ Princess Theatre
Houdini was sucker-punched here | 182

88___ Prison des Patriotes
Centuries of crime and punishment | 184

89___ Provigo Fortin Crane
A nod to our railway history | 186

90___ The Pullman Chandelier
Eye-catching effervescence | 188

91___ René Lévesque Park
A spectacular open-air oeuvre | 190

92___ The Roundhouse Café
Bannock, maple lattes, and more Indigenous treats | 192

93___ Royal Montreal Curling
More than two centuries of sweeping | 194

94___ The Saint-Léonard Cavern
The star of the speleological society | 196

95___ The Secret Towers House
This Old House | 198

96___ SOS Labyrinthe
Let's get lost | 200

97___ Spa Saint James
The distinctly Quebecois maple syrup massage | 202

98___ Square Saint-Louis
A neighbourhood affair | 204

99   Squirrelgoyles
Lovable little pests at the Mount Royal Chalet | 206

100   St. Joseph's Oratory
The beating heart of Mount Royal | 208

101   Surf the Saint Lawrence with KSF
Hang ten on Habs territory | 210

102   T&T Supermarket
The biggest Asian supermarket in Canada | 212

103   The Three Bares Fountain
A comedy of errors at the McGill University campus | 214

104   Twilight Sculpture Garden
One person's trash… | 216

105   Tyrolienne MTL Zipline
Come fly with me | 218

106   Verdun Beach
A day at the beach – in the city | 220

107   Westmount Lawn Bowling & Croquet Club
A social club on the green grass | 222

108   Westmount Public Library
Check out the postcard collection | 224

109   The Wheel Club
Hillbilly Night in the middle of the metropolis | 226

110   Wilensky's Light Lunch
The rules are the rules | 228

111   Windsor Station
The former hub for Canadian travel | 230

1 Acro Park Studio
Where clowning around is a requirement

What could possibly be more exhilarating than hanging suspended in the air while you twist and turn your way around, supported by your own body weight and a handful of silk ropes?

The Acro Park studio in Vaudreuil-Dorion pays homage to Montreal's rich circus history by making the tradition accessible to everyone who dreams of floating or twirling up in the air – and getting fit in the process. The family-friendly classes are run by expert circus artists and trainers and designed to help just about anyone conquer their fear of heights while getting in a pretty darn good workout in the process.

The small classes are meant to be intimate, allowing you to get ample supervision and time with your professional circus artist. Whether you're opting for aerial hoops, aerial straps, family-friendly kid circus classes, or even pole fitness, expect to find yourself barefoot and free of any harnesses or restraints. The goal of aerial circus is to work your upper body strength and core muscles to support yourself while moving in an elegant and *laissez-faire* fashion. But don't worry. These classes tend to draw the curious and amateurs, and the trainers are ready to cater to all skill levels.

Acro Park aims to change your perspective – both literally and figuratively – on what fitness and working out can look like, and also about the sheer volume of work that goes into being a circus performer, a profession that pays the bills for thousands of Montrealers living at home or working abroad. The boutique fitness studio offers a variety of different options depending on your unique interests, from one-day private training for recreation to recurring classes for artists and professional athletes.

Those who prefer staying comfortably at ground level should note that Acro Park also offers performances by professional aerial artists and students alike, an affordable and informative way to understand Montreal aerial circus arts on an intimate level.

Address 3650 Boulevard de la Cité-des-Jeunes, No. 103, Vaudreuil-Dorion, QC J7V 8P2, +1 (514) 910-8234, www.acropark.ca, acroparkstudio@gmail.com | Getting there By car, take the Autoroute 40 W to Exit 32 Boulevard de la Cité-des-Jeunes. Venue will be on your right. | Hours See website for class schedule and booking information | Tip At the centre of Circus Arts City, see professional acrobats perform at Tohu (2345 Rue Jarry E, www.tohu.ca/en). The circular theatre hosts local and visiting artists, clowns, acrobats, and more.

2 Allan Memorial Institute

Dark history hidden in plain sight

The Allan Memorial Institute in the Golden Square Mile might look like a dazzling Italian Renaissance mansion on the outside, but the property has one of the most disturbing pasts in the city's modern history. Built in 1860 by Scottish Canadian businessman Sir Hugh Allan, the 72-room mansion known as Ravenscrag was considered at the time to surpass in size and cost any existing residence in the country, with its intentionally imposing and intimidating interior and exterior décor that were designed to host some of the most important political and social events of the era.

The sprawling mansion rests upon a gentle slope on Mount Royal and overlooks what is now the downtown McGill University campus. The enormous size and downtown location made it one of the most desirable addresses in the city, and it was eventually donated to the Royal Victoria Hospital in 1940 by Sir Allan's second son, Sir Montagu Allan, with the intention that the property would become a medical research center.

Here's where things get dark. The research center was taken over by the CIA between 1957 and 1964, when, in collaboration with psychiatrist Donald Ewen Cameron, the agency conducted Project MKUltra. The illegal human experimentation program involved psychological torture, sexual abuse, electroshock, and ingestion of psychoactive drugs on unwitting Canadian and US citizens in an attempt to find the best methods to force confessions through brainwashing and psychological torture during interrogations.

The storied building currently functions as a much more respected institution and can only be viewed from the outside. Although the building hasn't fully shed its dark history, the institute is currently in the hands of the McGill University Faculty of Medicine and is used for outpatient psychiatric services in collaboration with the Montreal General Hospital.

Address 1025 Avenue Pine W, Montreal, QC H3A 1A1 | Getting there Metro 1 to McGill (Green Line), then walk 15 minutes; bus 144, 360 or 107 to Des Pins/Peel | Hours Unrestricted from the outside only | Tip The nearby Maude Abbott Medical Museum (Strathcona Anatomy and Dentistry Building, 3640 Rue University, Room 2/38E, www.mcgill.ca/medicalmuseum) hosts a comprehensive collection of the materials and artifacts documenting McGill University's teaching hospitals throughout its history.

3 Alley Cat Gallery
A cat-focused public art institution

Blink and you might miss this guerilla art gallery in the heart of the NDG neighbourhood. Originally conceptualized to help deter illegal graffiti in a dimly lit neighbourhood alleyway, the Alley Cat Gallery consists of a charming and slightly kitschy mix of prints and reproductions of famous cat-themed paintings, as well as original feline-focused artworks by local artists and creatives.

The apartment complex courtyard is packed with various cat forms and still lifes from local artists such as James Duncan and Rupert Bottenberg, but nothing in this open-air gallery is for sale. According to the gallery's official cat-themed curator John Jordan, that would be missing the point entirely.

Jordan and his cat Humbert are the creative duo behind the Alley Cat Gallery, where many of the works are inspired by Humbert's antics. Jordan got the idea for the gallery when he first moved into the adjacent apartment complex back in 2008. While taking his cat out on a leash to enjoy a little fresh air, he spotted graffiti removal crews coming time and time again to remove unsightly tags from the building's brick façade. The duo spent so much time in the alleyway that Jordan began cleaning it up himself, sweeping away cigarette butts and bringing out potted plants to make the space a more welcoming outdoor area to spend time in.

It wasn't long after that when Jordan began slowly bringing out cat pictures and hanging them on the wall, a gesture he hoped his landlord wouldn't mind. The results speak for themselves. The quiet alleyway is now one of the most well-loved alleys in the neighbourhood with cat- and art-lovers stopping to take pictures on a daily basis. His landlord didn't mind, and Jordan's efforts have worked, for the most part, to deter unsightly tags and unwanted graffiti. The formerly forgotten alleyway continues to be a landmark institution in the neighbourhood.

Address 5711B Rue Sherbrooke W, Montreal, QC H4A 1W9, +1 (514) 475-3777, www.facebook.com/alleycatgallery514, osmosis@osmosisunlimited.com | Getting there Metro 2 to Vendôme (Orange Line), then walk 15 minutes; bus 105, 365 to Sherbrooke/Wilson | Hours Unrestricted | Tip The Café Chat L'Heureux (172 Avenue Duluth E, www.cafechatlheureux.com) is the very first cat café to open in North America, hosting eight friendly felines adopted from the SPCA and offering a comprehensive vegan-friendly food and drink menu.

4 Atrium Le 1000

Go skating in a skyscraper

Montreal is widely known as a snow-globe-worthy, winter wonderland. While that is true for a few months out of the year, it also has its greener months. But there's a place where winter-loving locals and visitors can experience the crisp chill of the cooler weather all year round. Located on the corner of Rue Mansfield and Rue De La Gauchetière W, Atrium Le 1000 is a year-round, indoor skating rink in the middle of the downtown core.

The stunning rink is on the main floor of the tallest building in the province, Le 1000 De La Gauchetière. This lively, wintery venue is set underneath a massive glass dome that allows the sun's rays to warm up air above the ice, creating a temperate and comfortable environment inside the full-sized arena. So you can happily step into a pair of skates and enjoy a few laps no matter what the weather is outside.

A curated playlist creates the fun and energized atmosphere here with pop hits and classic Quebecois tunes, all designed to foster an upbeat vibe for beginners and intermediate skaters alike to spend the day skating. Atrium Le 1000 also offers a handful of casual restaurants around the rink, and the food-court-style seating provides unparalleled vantage points of the rink below and the sun-flooded glass dome above. You and your skating friends can enjoy taking intermittent hot chocolate or poutine breaks and then heading back down to the ice.

It might feel a little unnatural to plan a trip to the skating rink when the temperature outside is well above freezing, but Le 1000 De La Gauchetière is actually one of the city's 133 LEED Certified Buildings. This means that the entire skyscraper, including the main floor skating rink, is energy efficient and sustainable. It uses fewer resources, including water and energy, while also generating less waste than the average building. So go ahead and lace up your skates!

Address 1000 Rue De La Gauchetière W, Montreal, QC H3B 4W5, +1 (514) 395-0555, www.le1000.com, atrium.le1000@groupepetra.com | Getting there Metro 2 to Bonaventure (Orange Line); bus 55, 86, 87 to Centre-Ville | Hours See website for skate times | Tip Go for a swim at the public pool at the Olympic Park underneath the Montreal Tower that hosted the '76 Olympic Games and continues to welcome swimmers of all skill levels for open swims and training sessions (3200 Rue Viau, www.parcolympique.qc.ca/centresportif/en).

5 Auberge du Dragon Rouge

Drink your way to medieval times

Montreal is known for its old-world architecture, such as the 1670s Le Ber-Le Moyne House or the 1687 Saint-Sulpice Seminary. But the Auberge du Dragon Rouge in the Villeray neighbourhood takes it all the way back to the Middle Ages. The kitsch pub and patio serve medieval-inspired dishes and drinks in an equally old-school setting that'll make you feel as though you've walked into a *Game of Thrones* set or perhaps the Great Hall in *Harry Potter*.

The Middle Ages-inspired restaurant commits to the theme, and patrons should be ready for a raucous dinner and a show. The wait-staff and kitchen crew double as actors and won't break character for your entire dining experience, which makes the entire evening equally immersive and comical all at once. Expect to see a performance that has been designed from start to finish specifically to take you many centuries back in time.

For more than twenty-five years, the Auberge du Dragon Rouge has been catering to guests who fancy all things medieval in an ultra-cozy atmosphere. You'll find it jam-packed with knights, barbarians, priests, innkeepers, and an entire cast of characters that look as if they've stepped out of the Middle Ages. With the music playing and the mead flowing, every night is different. The restaurant is always a little unpredictable, which entices people to come back over and over again.

The Auberge du Dragon Rouge retains the medieval theme on its menu, with dishes like "dragon trichobezoars" (fried onions) and spicy "dragon hatchling wings" flanking the menu. Gargantua's Platter is a great feast for two to twelve people. This legacy restaurant champions seasonal Quebecois ingredients. Look for the circular, yellow "Aliments du Québec" logo next to many selections and rest assured that, although your dining experience is inspired by the Middle Ages, it's certainly going to be fresh and locally sourced!

Address 8870 Rue Lajeunesse, Montreal, QC H2M 1R6, +1 (514) 858-5711 #221,
www.oyez.ca/aubergedudragonrouge, aubergedudragonrouge@oyez.ca | Getting there
Metro 2 to Crémazie (Orange Line); bus 54, 146 to Christophe-Colombe/Émile-
Journault | Hours See website for seatings | Tip If you want to dress the part, be
sure to make a pit stop at Boutique Médiévale Dracolite (6370 Rue Saint-Hubert,
www.boutiquemedievale.com), where you'll find period costumes inspired by the
Middle Ages, as well as plenty of replica memorabilia and collectables.

6   Auberge Saint Gabriel

Share a round of Shirley Temples with a ghost

No Montreal resident would compare the city to Paris – most turn their nose up to any comparison to Europe at all. But it's hard to not notice the distinct European architecture within the walls of the Old Port of Montreal, especially in the case at Auberge Saint Gabriel. The oldest auberge in Montreal, it was the first of its kind to receive a liquor license in North America.

Auberge Saint Gabriel was built in 1688 by French pioneer Etienne Truteau and houses more than 300 years of local and international history. In terms of modern North American history, this is about as old as it gets. The building has functioned as a townhouse, a fur trading post, the Beauchemin printing press operation, and eventually, a community space and speakeasy. And, like most centuries-old buildings, it is reported to have a permanent resident from the beyond.

The Old Montreal restaurant and bar has been rated the "most haunted" venue in the province time and time again. But don't worry – the consensus is that it's actually a pretty friendly ghost. Although there have been plenty of spooky sightings over the years, the most enduring local legend suggests that the auberge is allegedly home to the ghost of a little girl who perished in a building fire in the 19th century. She and her grandfather were trapped upstairs while he was teaching her to play the piano.

Visitors and patrons over the years have regularly reported hearing the little girl playing the piano when nobody else is around, while others have mentioned feeling an unexplained but not necessarily menacing, presence surrounding them. Although the venue now functions as one of the higher-end, modern restaurants in the Old Port, it's hard not to imagine the abundance of spirits and stories that the brick-lined walls and stained glass windows have witnessed over more than 300 years.

Address 426 Rue St Gabriel, Montreal, QC H2Y 2Z9, +1 (514) 878-3561,
www.aubergesaint-gabriel.com/en, info@aubergesaint-gabriel.com | Getting there
Metro 2 to Place-d'Armes (Orange Line); bus 129 to Saint-Antoine/Champ-de-Mars |
Hours Tue–Fri 5–10:30pm | Tip Navette Maritime ferry (Rue de la Commune Est,
www.navettesfluviales.com) from the nearby Jacques-Cartier Pier takes you across the
water to Île Sainte-Hélène in less than 10 minutes and costs less than a latte.

7 __ Bain Morgan

Beaux Art bathhouse

Bain Morgan was considered to be one of the most beautiful examples of Beaux-Arts style architecture in the city during its 1916 unveiling. The community space was a shining example of how public-focused buildings could still offer style and flair without sacrificing functionality and pragmatism. The East End bathhouse was originally erected over a hundred years ago to allow city dwellers of all statuses and walks of life to take care of their personal hygiene in a dignified fashion, which meant that residents of Maisonneuve, a city distinct from Montreal back in the early 1900s, would no longer have to scrounge for bathing facilities or, more commonly, forego bathing entirely.

It might have been conceived to benefit people with limited resources, but the city of Maisonneuve spared no expense in constructing the public bathhouse. Bain Morgan was designed to look just like Grand Central Station in New York City, complete with limestone columns and copper window and door frames. The opulent bathhouse was considered a major success, but Maisonneuve ran into financial problems a few short years later. The city was eventually annexed to Montreal, and it remains one of the city's easternmost boroughs to this day.

Although personal hygiene has more or less moved from the public bathhouse into our private bathrooms for most of us, Bain Morgan retains a part of its history as a public, indoor swimming pool and gymnasium that is, well, way more stunning than it has a right to be! The Mercier–Hochelaga-Maisonneuve neighbourhood pool is completely free for the public to use, with a generous open-swim schedule that includes both adults-only swimming and child-friendly swims as well. Bain Morgan might function mainly as a public pool, but there are still showers and bathing facilities available to wash off the chlorine after a few refreshing laps.

Address 1875 Avenue Morgan, Montreal, QC H1V 2R1, +1 (514) 872-6657 | Getting there Metro 1 to Pie-IX (Green Line); bus 125 to Ontario/William-David | Hours See website for open swim times | Tip The Seed Library at the Bibliothèque Maisonneuve, a striking Beaux Arts library that dates back over a century, is a special collection of free and ready-to-plant seeds curated for their ability to flourish on urban balconies (4120 Rue Ontario Est, www.montreal.ca/en/places/bibliotheque-maisonneuve).

8__ The Barbie Expo

The world's largest Barbie doll exhibition

If you grew up racing up and down the bubble-gum pink Barbie aisle in the toy store, then the Barbie Expo at Les Cours Mont-Royal will absolutely delight your inner child. Be prepared to gaze upon classic and special edition Barbie dolls around each and every corner.

You might not expect to see such a chic setup just outside of the Peel Metro station. The venue looks more like a high-end, walk-in closet or design studio than a toy store. The Barbie Expo is the largest permanent exhibition of Barbie dolls in the entire world, featuring more than a thousand different Barbies. There are one-of-a-kind Barbies, and celebrity Barbies are well represented, including timeless icons like Audrey Hepburn, Lucille Ball, and Beyoncé. Look for the dolls wearing garments created by some of the most coveted fashion designers in the world, including Christian Dior, Donna Karan, Oscar de la Renta, Vera Wang, Bob Mackie, and Byron Lars, among other luminaries of the fashion world. Barbies here also represent the arts, sports, and much, much more.

According to Valerie Law, Vice-President of Marketing at the Soltron Group, which owns both Les Cours Mont-Royal and Barbie Expo, the exhibit space is about more than just Barbie herself. It's a celebration and a time capsule showcasing the many trends and styles that have graced the runway and the toy aisle since Barbie first hit the scene in 1959. It's all just on a much smaller scale, and Barbie's iconic appeal just keeps growing.

This unique exposition and snapshot-in-time gets even better because it's completely free to visit, not just for children but for adults as well. That being said, the high-end doll collection does accept donations for Make-A-Wish Quebec, the organization that grants wishes to local children and teenagers with critical illnesses. Before you leave, step inside the Instagram-friendly, life-sized doll box, and turn yourself into your very own Barbie.

Address 1455 Rue Peel, Suite 206, Montreal, QC H3A 1T5, +1 (514) 380-3830, www.expobarbie.ca | Getting there Metro 1 to Peel (Green Line) or Metro 2 to Bonaventure (Orange Line); bus 15, 107 to Peel | Hours Mon–Wed 10am–6pm, Thu & Fri 10am–9pm, Sat 10am–5pm, Sun noon–5pm | Tip Part workshop, part toy store, La Grande Ourse (263 Avenue Duluth E, www.lagrandeourse.jimdofree.com) is packed with locally made toys and games and also offers a variety of tutorials and lessons for kids young and old looking to make their own hand-crafted treasures.

9 __ Bed-In for Peace
John & Yoko slept here

You may not associate the City of Montreal with John Lennon and Yoko Ono, but on May 26, 1969, Suite 1742 at the Fairmont The Queen Elizabeth Hotel became the site of the second Bed-In for Peace, following the first one held earlier that year at the Amsterdam Hilton Hotel. The newlyweds staged these nonviolent protests in response to the raging Vietnam War.

The second Bed-In for Peace was originally supposed to take place in New York City, but due to a cannabis conviction the year prior, Lennon was denied entry into the US. Montreal was the obvious next choice, as its close proximity to New York facilitated more New York media coverage. John and Yoko, alongside a whole slew of journalists and reporters spread out on the floor, spent the next week essentially doing a press event from bed as a way to promote world peace. Lennon also recorded a little song known as "Give Peace a Chance" in this very room.

Today, the suite is still available for Beatles fans to book. The carefully preserved block of rooms was converted into one big suite packed with authentic memorabilia from the event, including documentation of the various noise complaints the hotel received from neighbouring guests. If you don't have the willpower to drop $3,000+/night to book the historic suite – don't sweat it. The 17th-floor hallway leading to the suite is outfitted with imagery from the week-long bed-in. You can also see the replica "Hair Peace" and "Bed Peace" signs on the windows from on the corner of Rue Mansfield and René Lévesque Boulevard.

On its 40th anniversary, the Bed-In for Peace was honoured at the Rue Peel entrance to Mount Royal Park with a subtle art intervention by artist Linda Covit and landscape architect Marie-Claude Séguin that consists of 180 rectangular limestone flagstones with "Give Peace a Chance" written and translated into forty different languages.

Address 900 Boulevard René-Lévesque W, Montreal, QC H3B 4A5, +1 (514) 861-3511, www.fairmont.com/queen-elizabeth-montreal, queenelizabeth.hotel@fairmont.com | Getting there Metro 2 to Bonaventure or Square-Victoria OACI (Orange Line); bus 350, 355, 358, 364 to René-Lévesque/Mansfield | Hours Unrestricted from the outside; see website for reservations | Tip Fairmont The Queen Elizabeth Hotel rests on top of the Montreal Central Station (895 Rue de la Gauchetière W, www.garecentrale.ca), where you can visit the art deco friezes inside and outside of the train station.

10 Berlin Wall Segment

Poetic spot for a heavy piece of history

Ruelle des Fortifications outside of the Old Port of Montreal is not often the first example of a North American fortification that comes to mind. But the City of Montreal was indeed protected by a series of wooden stockades and eventually a stone wall from 1685 until 1812, when fortification no longer made sense for an expanding city centre. The wall was demolished to make room for the burgeoning Financial District.

Fortunately, the Ruelle des Fortifications was conserved and protected and can still be visited within the World Trade Centre, where the glassed-in, stone atrium offers a convergence of past and present. The light-flooded alleyway is packed with shops, restaurants, and artwork, but visions of the past are easy to conjure up, thanks to the preserved brick structures.

It's fitting, then, that the World Trade Centre in the middle of the Old Port and the Quartier international neighbourhoods has also become home to a wall of another kind. Gifted to the City of Montreal from the City of Berlin to commemorate Montreal's 350th Anniversary in 1992, a segment of the Berlin Wall is now on view on Ruelle des Fortifications, a particularly poetic location where Montreal's own former fortification wall once stood.

The colourful segment is but one piece of the famous wall that separated West Berlin from East Berlin beginning in 1961. The Berlin Wall finally came down on November 9, 1989 during the Peaceful Revolution that resulted in the opening of East Germany's borders. Despite the segment's historical and cultural significance, though, no museums in Montreal were interested in receiving the gift due to its sheer size, as it weighs more than two tonnes and stands at 3.6 metres (12 feet) tall and 1.2 metres (4 feet) wide. It took the city three years to find an appropriate spot that would do it justice and also provide enough protection from the elements.

Address 747 Rue du Square-Victoria, Montreal, QC H2Y 3Y9, www.artpublicmontreal.ca |
Getting there Metro 1 to Place-des-Arts (Green Line) or Metro 2 to Square Victoria-
OACI (Orange Line) | Hours Mon–Fri 9am–5pm, Sat & Sun noon–5pm | Tip For more
German culture in Montreal, head to Boucherie Atlantique (5060 Chemin de la Côte-
des-Neiges, www.boucherieatlantique.ca), a family-run deli and specialty shop that stocks
various goods, sweets, and imports flown in directly from Germany and Austria.

11 Bison Bust at Joe Beef

An unsuspected bathroom attendant

The infamous Joe Beef restaurant in Little Burgundy is one of those elusive eateries in the city that everybody knows about, but most have not actually dined there. One reason for this situation is that the Anthony Bourdain-approved institution is always booked up weeks and sometimes months in advance. And the curtained and tchotchke-filled windows make it an almost intimidating feat to suss out what you'll find if you get the chance to step inside the recessed doors.

Let's get one thing out of the way immediately: there's a reason Joe Beef has remained at the top of every "Best Of" list for Montreal and beyond. The restaurant is responsible for a shift in dining preferences in the city. Its locally sourced and seasonal chalkboard menu, combined with a focus on natural and organic wine, along with its championing of Quebec winemakers, changed the way Quebecers and travellers look at the bounty that the province has to offer.

The restaurant might be touted for its curated menu and wine list, but it's hard not to notice the abundance of cheeky decor and accessories that make the space feel more like a countryside chalet than one of the most sophisticated restaurants in Canada. You'll instantly be taken by the old-timey landscape paintings, fish motifs, and whimsical souvenirs … until you excuse yourself for a bathroom break, that is.

Montreal isn't known for its bathroom attendants the way many cities in Europe and around the world are – except maybe at Joe Beef. Lock yourself in the bathroom after a glass of wine or two and be prepared to stare down a full-sized, taxidermy bison bust mounted on the wall and watching over you as you do your business. The toilet paper dispenser might also come as a shock: each roll of toilet paper is held up by the supportive horns of a ceramic bull bust, always at the ready to offer you some squares of tissue.

Address 2491 Rue Notre-Dame W, Montreal, QC H3J 1N6, +1 (514) 935-6504, www.joebeef.com | **Getting there** Metro 2 to Lionel-Groulx (Orange Line) | **Hours** Tue–Sat 5–10:30pm | **Tip** Follow the Lachine Canal to the Canal Lounge (Quai Atwater, www.canallounge.com), a cozy, stationary boat-turned-bar that serves up drinks and snacks juxtaposed against stunning views of the canal waterways and the neighbouring Atwater Market.

12 Cabaret Lion d'Or
Century-old entertainment

There are dozens of spectacular historic performance venues throughout Montreal, which arguably makes the show or performance that much more memorable, when the venue itself is a big part of the experience. But there's something particularly special about the monochromatic, red-hued Cabaret Lion d'Or, an art deco performance venue that has been welcoming guests in for an evening of entertainment since it first opened its doors on Rue Ontario nearly a century ago.

Cabaret Lion d'Or is the only remaining cabaret from the 1930s left in Montreal. The bright-colored space instantly transports its guests to a long-forgotten era of Montreal society – at least for the night. But don't expect to experience a stunning cabaret up close. Although the venue has been carefully preserved, you won't find traditional cabaret performances here. Instead, the Cabaret Lion d'Or of present-day currently functions mainly as a jazz and blues club with regular performances from visiting and local favourites.

The venue was conceived and conceptualized by Madame Leda Duhamel, the administrator behind Hotel Papineau. The construction workers assigned to the building of the Jacques Cartier Bridge stayed in the hotel during the project. As the project came to an end, she decided to open a cabaret in the same building to diversify her clientele and create a more sophisticated offering. Two new floors were added to the hotel directly above the newly opened Cabaret Lion d'Or.

While visiting the venue, you'll want to look up and soak in all the details and points of visual interest that go beyond what's playing on stage that night. Cabaret Lion d'Or has carefully preserved much of the original detailing and decor led by Madame Duhamel. Look for the original 1920s-era chandeliers that are still hanging from the ceilings throughout the venue – they are the standout feature here.

Address 1676 Rue Ontario E, Montreal, QC H2L 1S7, www.cabaretliondor.com, +1 (514) 598-0709, info@cabaretliondor.com | Getting there Metro 1 to Papineau (Green Line); bus 45, 359, 445 to Papineau/Ontario | Hours See website for showtimes | Tip Parc du Pied-du-Courant (2380 Rue Notre-Dame E, www.aupiedducourant.ca) is the outdoor area underneath the Jacques Cartier Bridge that is always bustling with a lively beer garden, food trucks, local artists, and community-focused events.

13__Cabaret Mado

Sparkle at this gender-bending institution

Want to know the best way to get to know the Gay Village and Montreal's LGBTQIA+ scene in a single evening? Then make a beeline directly to Cabaret Mado any night of the week. The cabaret drag bar owned by Montreal-based drag queen Mado Lamotte has been drawing in crowds from the local community and beyond for over 20 years and continues to be one of the most fabulous and welcoming destinations between Beaudry and Papineau.

To say that Mado Lamotte is a local legend would simply not be giving her enough credit. The drag queen, author, and entrepreneur has been performing in Montreal for well over 30 years. She began her drag career in the late 1980s and eventually became MC and DJ of Ciel Mon Mardi at Sky Bar before opening Cabaret Mado in 2002. These days, Mado will typically perform an opening song before retiring to the DJ booth for the night and setting the stage for local and one-off visiting queens to steal the show.

Cabaret Mado offers a sparkling snapshot into the thriving Gay Village in Montreal. Walk through the front door – you can't miss it, thanks to Mado's larger-than-life likeness adorning the marquee above the entryway – and prepare yourself for an evening of laughter and fun. Whether it's a live viewing party of *RuPaul's Drag Race,* a 1920s-inspired burlesque show, or a sequin-emblazoned tribute to Celine Dion or Lady Gaga, you're guaranteed a memorable time.

Although a fan favourite within the Village, Cabaret Mado is actually a very intimate space with limited seating, so if you're planning on catching a show, you'll want to arrive early enough to snag a comfortable seat. Choose your spot wisely though because if you're one of the brave patrons who choose to occupy the front few rows next to the stage – not unlike a comedy show – you're going to want to be prepared and happy to endure some gentle heckling and teasing throughout the performance!

Address 1115 Rue Sainte-Catherine E, Montreal, QC H2L 2G2, +1 (514) 525-7566, www.mado.qc.ca | Getting there Metro 1 to Beaudry (Green Line) or Metro 1, 2, 4 to Berri-UQAM (Green, Orange, Yellow Lines) | Hours Daily 4pm–3am, see website for show schedule | Tip Beaudry Metro Station features rainbow-hued public art designed to mark the beginning of the Village, the heart of Montreal's gay scene, which spans between Beaudry and Papineau.

14 Camillien-Houde Lookout

Panoramic views and paranormal activity

The Camillien-Houde Lookout is one of the most popular spots for taking in views of Montreal below. Named after Camellien Houde (1889–1958), a politician who served as mayor of Montreal for four terms, it's one of the first places out-of-towners flock to take in the lay of the land and snap a selfie with the unobstructed cityscape below. There's no denying that this popular lookout is one of the city's most visually stunning destinations, but there's a lot more to the viewpoint than meets the eye.

The mountaintop destination is relatively easy to get to, thanks to its position on the northeastern slope of Mont-Royal, and as such draws in thousands of tourists and locals each year, but not many people know that the site is allegedly home to some serious paranormal activity. The lookout borders the notoriously haunted Mont-Royal Cemetery, and many visiting and local site-seers have reported strange sightings and inexplicable activity and goings-on throughout the years.

The Camillien-Houde Lookout first opened to the public in 1958 and quickly charmed the city's residents with its winding staircases, art-deco lamp posts, and plenty of spots to perch and get cozy with a loved one while enjoying the sights and sounds of the city from above. But it has also seen its fair share of accidents, including multiple cases of people falling down the steep steps.

Although the site is much safer now, as railings and barriers have been put in place, it has become commonplace for those visiting the "Lover's Lookout" to report sightings of the undead. One spirit is the alleged ghost of an Algonquian warrior, who has been the most commonly reported sighting over the years. There have also been reports of theft of food and drinks among sightseers, but that's largely due to the large population of cute but mischievous raccoons that roam Mont-Royal come nightfall!

Address Voie Camillien-Houde, Montreal, QC H2W 1S8 | Getting there Bus 11, 711 to Belvédère Camillien-Houde | Hours Daily 6am–11pm | Tip Tucked into the tippy-top of Place Ville Marie, Les Enfants Terribles restaurant towers above the city on the 44th floor with unobstructed views and an excellent breakfast poutine (entrance at 1 Boulevard Robert-Bourassa, www.jesuisunenfantterrible.com/place-ville-marie).

15 Canada Malting Co.

Urban exploration on the banks of the Lachine Canal

Some consider it an eyesore, while others think it to be the Mount Everest of urban exploration in Montreal. Whichever way you slice it, the remaining Canada Malting Co. buildings on the banks of the Lachine Canal provide a commanding presence on the trendy Saint Henri neighbourhood skyline.

The Canada Malting Co. complex was first constructed in 1904 by Montreal architect David Jerome Spence. It functioned as a malting factory for distilleries and breweries until the early 1980s, when the Lachine Canal closed and forced companies to transport goods via railway rather than by water. The property was then temporarily used to store soya and corn before being completely abandoned only a few years later. By 1989, the ancient clay silos had little commercial use and have been left abandoned and deteriorating to this day.

That being said, the cultural importance of the eleven buildings and silos is not lost on local historians. The complex has now been designated as part of the Lachine Canal National Historic Site, which protects them from being demolished without reason. Unfortunately, the status doesn't protect them from natural decay or vandalism. It's too expensive to enlist full-time security for the perimeter of the building, and the site has become an urban explorer's playground.

The interior of the buildings is reportedly in a deep state of disrepair, and while people sometimes trespass inside the condemned buildings, you can see the site legally, safely, and clearly from the street. The gigantic, 46-metre (150-foot) silo buildings are always buzzing with fresh graffiti by local and visiting artists, which can be quite the sight to see from the comfort of the sidewalk. Look for the mysteriously pink house perched atop the tallest building in the complex. Nobody knows who is behind it, but they decorate the little structure for every holiday.

Address 5020-5070 Rue Saint-Ambroise, Montreal, QC H4C 2G1, www.heritagemontreal.org/en/site/canada-malting-co | Getting there Bus 191 to Notre-Dame/Saint-Rémi | Hours Unrestricted from the outside only | Tip Continue walking along the Lachine Canal to the McAuslan Brasserie & Distillerie (5080 Rue St Ambroise, www.mcauslan.com/la-brasserie/visite-de-la-brasserie). The pay-what-you-can brewery tour will get you a complimentary beer tasting with proceeds going to Mission Bon Accueil.

16 CCA Garden
Public art and plenty of people-watching

Well loved by architecture aficionados and neighbourhood students looking for a covert spot to crack a beer under the sun, the Canadian Centre for Architecture (CCA) Garden is perched in the middle of two highway ramps and a train track. This might not sound like the most glamorous spot for an outdoor museum, but its urban location suits the distinct industrial design perfectly.

The outdoor, public space is considered by the CCA to be half open-air museum and half garden tucked into the south side of René-Lévesque Boulevard just across the street from the CCA's main buildings. It was designed with the intention of creating a space that helps to foster the integration of art and architecture for public use, and it has succeeded in doing just that.

The City of Montreal granted the site to the CCA over thirty years ago in 1986, and it was placed in the hands of Melvin Charney, the esteemed Montreal-based artist-architect, who transformed the space into an accessible park in the middle of the city centre. He created a green space for the public to partake in art appreciation without pretension or admission fees.

Charney's compelling garden is intended to walk visitors through a series of narrative episodes that represent the history of the city and its surrounding architecture by way of whimsical obelisks, or "allegorical columns" as Charney calls them, which is a series of inanimate objects, including a lone metal chair and a copper Roman temple, that extend toward the sky overlooking the Saint Henri neighbourhood below.

It took Charney over 10 years to transform the space from traffic island to public park and while the somewhat ludicrous sculptures were designed to represent the ever-changing Montreal skyline, the slightly sloping positioning of the garden makes the location itself an unbeatable spot to stop and reflect on the city from above.

Address 1920 Rue Baile, Montreal, QC H3H 2S6, +1 (514) 939-7026, www.cca.qc.ca, accueil@cca.qc.ca | Getting there Metro 1 to Guy-Concordia (Green Line) or Metro 2 to Lucien-L'Allier (Orange Line) | Hours Unrestricted | Tip Make your way to the Leonard & Bina Ellen Art Gallery (1400 Boulevard Maisonneuve W, ellengallery.concordia.ca), the contemporary art space within Concordia University offering a rotating buffet of Canadian and Québécois art designed to promote greater awareness of art as a way to engage in political and cultural commentary on a local and international level.

17 Centre Toussaint
Cooking, Creole, and Haitian history

You can't talk about historic and present-day Montreal without talking about Haitian culture. Of course, the city is a veritable melting pot of well-defined communities and cultures across the board, but the Haitian diaspora is represented throughout the city.

"Personally, I feel that the Haitian community has a great impact on Montreal's culture, from our food, the music we dance to, and to our language," Harvin Hilaire, Former VP of External Affairs for the Haitian Students' Association of Concordia told *The Haitian Times*. "You can see that a lot of our culture has been adapted by other communities in Montreal."

Sly Toussaint recognized the need for a community centre dedicated to the Haitian impact in Montreal, and that's exactly what drove her to open Centre Toussaint in the Ahuntsic-Cartierville neighbourhood after returning from Port-au-Prince in 2008. The learning enrichment centre promotes personal wellness and Haitian culture by teaching Haitian Creole, folk dance, history, and cooking classes, all designed to foster personal growth and a greater understanding of the Afro and Haitian experience in Montreal.

Interested in figuring out all the techniques and spices that go into your favourite Haitian dish? Keen to learn to speak Creole to impress your Haitian friends or communicate better with loved ones? Maybe you're just looking for a class that'll open your mind to new forms of creative expression. Whatever your motivation, Centre Toussaint recognizes the importance of blending a fun and uplifting experience with actionable knowledge and takeaways.

The Centre Toussaint also offers drop-in and à la carte options for those who want to get a better taste of Haitian culture without committing to a regular schedule. Most drop-in classes take place in March, June, September, and December, and specialized private lessons are also available upon request.

Address 2865 Rue Fleury E, Montreal, QC H2B 1M1, +1 (438) 771-5507, www.centretoussaint.com/en, info@centretoussaint.com | Getting there Bus 140 to Fleury/ Larose | Hours See website for class schedule | Tip Also in the Ahunstic neighbourhood is the Parc-nature de l'Île-de-la-Visitation (2425 Boulevard Gouin E), a nature reserve with bike paths and barbecue pits in the summer and long waterfront trails ripe for birdwatching.

18 Céramic Café Studio
Colour me happy

We could all use a little extra dose of serotonin and relaxation these days, which is probably why the Céramic Café Studio has continued to draw in clientele of all ages and interests since its inception over 20 years ago.

The colourful ceramic studio first opened its doors in Montreal back in 1997, when owners Gilles Geoffrion and Paola Cacopardo decided they would create a space where young people and anyone wishing to explore their creative side could gather. Today, you'll find nothing but encouragement and a strong sense of community in this low-stakes, judgement-free zone. If you want to stoke your artistic flames to see what you can create with your own hands, this is the place to do it.

The best part about the Céramic Café Studio is that it's geared toward all walks of life. You don't have to bring a group of kids if you want to test your hand at painting your own ceramics, but kids of all ages are certainly welcome. Geoffrion and Cacopardo have helped all kinds of people get in on the action, from bachelorette parties and kids' birthdays to celebrities like Charlotte Gainsbourg and Véronique Cloutier.

Céramic Café Studio provides everything you could possibly need to foster your inner *artiste,* including helpful artistic consultants available at all times to provide advice and suggestions while you get your paint on. The studio also doubles as a fully equipped restaurant, so you can refuel as you go. The panini is a favourite menu item – it's somewhat famous and you'll see why!

After you've carefully painted your ceramics and perhaps indulged in a little treat from the café, your artistic consultant will take care of the finishing touches so that your ceramics will really shine. Your unique piece of art will be whisked away to be dried and fired inside the onsite kiln for 24 hours. When you see it again, it'll be glossy and ready to be cherished.

Address 4338 Rue Saint Denis, Montreal, QC H2J 2K8, +1 (514) 848-1119, www.leccs.com, montreal@leccs.com | Getting there Metro 1 to Mont-Royal (Orange Line) | Hours Mon–Wed 10am–11pm, Thu–Sat 10am–midnight, Sun 10am–10pm | Tip Take your creativity straight to the source by learning to make your own pottery at Atelier Cône10 (3941 Saint Denis, www.cone10.ca), a studio that teaches the art of pottery-making from the wheel to the kiln.

19__Cheap Thrills Records

The wonky purple stairway to music heaven

Climbing up the slightly crooked and menacing stairway to Cheap Thrills Records is akin to falling into the rabbit hole in *Alice in Wonderland,* or stepping into a Beatles melody circa *Sgt. Pepper's Lonely Hearts Club Band.* The purple-hued, gravity-defying staircase is akin to a funhouse entrance as it leads eager audiophiles up to what most vinyl-loving Montrealers consider to be the beating heart, or perhaps the very father, of all record stores in the city.

The unassuming downtown address first opened its doors decades ago in 1971 and is considered to be the first and largest record store in Montreal. Unlike a lot of vinyl and specialty listening shops, this humble record store is instantly welcoming. Visitors immediately feel at ease and comfortable enough to look for or request anything from Miles Davis and Duke Ellington to the latest Taylor Swift and Lizzo releases. You'll find no judgment here: your taste is your taste, and it's perfectly valid.

You could easily spend hours digging through the diverse selection of vinyl both new and vintage. The impressive inventory at Cheap Thrills clocks in at well over 10,000 titles ranging from metal and punk to hip hop and blues, and pretty much everything in between. Once you're satisfied with your selection of LPs, head to the back of the store, where pop-culture aficionados will find their treasures. This area is reserved for retro items, including cassettes, CDs, and a delicious selection of used and vintage books, from vintage travel guides to literary classics.

With absolutely no frills or pretension in stock at Cheap Thrills, you'll be taken by the hand-written signage written in permanent marker on pieces of cardboard, the walls covered with a mismatched gallery of show promotions and band posters, and dangling Edison bulbs that evoke a sense of nostalgia for your high school bedroom in the very best way.

Address 2044 Rue Metcalfe, 2nd Floor, Montreal, QC H3A 1X8, +1 (514) 844-8988, www.cheapthrills.ca, info@cheapthrills.ca | Getting there Metro 1 to Peel (Green Line) | Hours Sun–Wed noon–5pm, Thu & Fri noon–7pm, Sat noon–6pm | Tip Check out BBAM! Gallery (808 Avenue Atwater, www.bbamgallery.com), a cozy, no-nonsense vinyl store set within a contemporary art gallery, with regular visual art expositions and live music in St. Henri.

20 Cinema L'Amour
A safe space to get your juices flowing

Where can you go to watch adult-themed films in a public movie house? While it might sound sticky or icky at first, Cinema L'Amour has created a community and safe space for indulging in fantasy alone or as a couple. Dating back to 1981, the kinky little theatre is the oldest entertainment venue of its kind in Montreal. The Plateau pornography cinema might have a lot going on behind closed doors, but this bright yellow-hued neighbourhood venue is an institution, something that Plateau residents walk by once, maybe twice a day without batting an eye.

Cinema L'Amour prides itself on being a welcoming space for everyone looking to indulge in kink-themed films. However, the intimate venue has no tolerance for disrespect or unwanted advances on its patrons. All mature adults over the age of 18 who are comfortable with the concept of enjoying theatrical pornography in public are welcomed, but there are a few things to keep in mind when frequenting this storied entertainment venue.

The upstairs horseshoe balconies of this cinema of love are reserved for couples, while the main level is open for general admission. Many regulars go to see and be seen enjoying themselves, which is allowed, but there are no rules that say that clients must partake in explicit extracurriculars. In fact, there are plenty of regular patrons who go to simply enjoy a taboo film in a tolerant environment.

The family behind Cinema L'Amour has been running the show since the beginning. The venue was originally constructed over a century ago in 1914, when it opened as an independent movie house and theatre hall with an emphasis on Yiddish films. Although the cinema has changed hands and concepts multiple times over the course of more than a hundred years, the ornate venue is still considered one of the most well-preserved and aesthetically stunning movie houses in the city.

Address 4015 Boulevard Saint-Laurent, Montreal, QC H2W 1Y4, +1 (514) 849-6227, www.cinemalamour.com/en, info@cinemalamour.com | Getting there Metro 2 to Mont-Royal (Orange Line); bus 29, 55, 363 to Saint-Laurent/Duluth | Hours Daily 11am–11pm, see website for showtimes | Tip Walk across the street to Bar Blue Dog (3958 Boulevard Saint-Laurent, www.facebook.com/TheBlueDogMotel), a dive bar and barbershop where you can get a haircut by day and catch an amateur comedy show or cut loose on the dance floor by night.

21 Comedy Nest
Get your laugh on – for less

Montreal's Just For Laughs is the internationally acclaimed comedy club and host of the comedy festival of the same name, but most comedy fiends have no idea that they can find the Comedy Nest just a few blocks away. The intimate comedy club hosts amateur comedians twice a week and offers free tickets to more well-known shows later in the week as an incentive for the audience to come out and support everyday community members hoping to test their funny bone.

The late Ernie Butler founded the Comedy Nest, originally known as Stitches, in 1979, with the intention of creating an affordable and relatively welcoming space to showcase the best in professional and amateur comedy in the city. Whether you're coming out for the newbie nights where "people with day jobs" take their first steps into the world of stand-up, or you're in the audience of the "comedy lab" where pro-amateurs and local comedians test out new jokes on the crowd, you're in for a night of laughter.

Don't let the name fool you either. The intimate comedy venue has seen some of the biggest names in the funny business since its inception and continues to welcome major headliners on a regular basis alongside its amateur and newbie roster. Household names ranging from Jim Carrey and Russell Peters to Debra DiGiovanni and Harland Williams have all graced the compact comedy stage over the years.

Although the club has changed hands and moved venues a couple of times over its lifespan, these days it's located on an unassuming passageway in the Montreal Forum (where the Montreal Canadiens famously won 24 Stanley Cups). The wheelchair-accessible comedy club holds just 160 patrons, and doors open about 45 minutes before showtime, which will allow you to cozy up with a couple of bar snacks or a cheap pint of beer before getting your laugh on for the evening for just a few dollars. Most shows cost less than $6 per person.

Address 2313 Rue Saint-Catherine W, Montreal, QC H3H 1N2 +1 (514) 932-6378, www.comedynest.com/shows | Getting there Metro 1 to Atwater (Green Line); bus 66 to Le Boulevard/De Trafalgar | Hours See website for showtimes | Tip Zigzag your way across the hall to the Forum Sports Bar & GamesCentre (2313 Rue Sainte-Catherine O, 4th Floor, www.forum-montreal.com/games-centre-arcades-billiards), where you'll find more than 75 classic arcade games, billiard tables, shuffleboard, and a fully functional bowling alley.

22 — Copernicus Monument

An ode to the Polish astronomer and mathematician

Polish-born Nicolaus Copernicus was a Renaissance-era mathematician and astronomer, and although he, arguably, might not be a household name outside of the science community, his contribution to 16th-century astronomy is unmatched. Copernicus was the first European scientist to propose that the Sun was in fact stationary in the centre of the universe and that the Earth revolved around it. The heliocentric theory of the solar system was considered radical at a time when most people believed that Earth was at the centre.

So, how did a monument dedicated to Nicolaus Copernicus end up on permanent display in Montreal? The bronze and concrete statue was originally acquired by the City of Montreal for Expo '67 and was relocated rather poetically to Chaboillez Square before ending up at its current location outside of the Rio Tinto Alcan de Montréal Planetarium in 2013.

But there's a bit more to the story. The statue was completed in 1966, and it is the brainchild of Bertel Thorvaldsen, a Danish sculptor born over 200 years ago. Thorvaldsen is the artist behind the identical and original Copernicus monument in Warsaw. The statue on display in Montreal is actually one of just two true replicas in the world. This one is the first posthumously cast bronze impression made using the same plaster mould from the original statue conserved at the Thorvaldsen Museum in Copenhagen.

Both the original and this true replica of the 19th-century monument depict Copernicus as accurately as possible. In order to give the statue an authentic face, Thorvaldsen based the statue on a series of Copernicus' self-portraits. His hair and clothing are accurate to common Polish fashions at the time. He holds a compass and armillary sphere in his hands as an ode to his radical heliocentric theory as he beckons visitors into the planetarium today.

Address 4801 Avenue Pierre-de Coubertin, Montreal, QC H1V 3J3, +1 (514) 868-3000, www.espacepourlavie.ca/planetarium | Getting there Metro 1 to Viau (Green Line); bus 185, 364 to Sherbrooke/No. 4751 | Hours Unrestricted | Tip The IMAX®TELUS Theatre at the Montreal Science Centre (2 Rue de la Commune W, www.montrealsciencecentre.com) shows cutting-edge science documentaries and education-focused films on the giant screen.

23__ Crew Collective & Café

Become the main character

There's no shortage of stunning coffee shops in Montreal. You'll find light-flooded and plant-filled cafés that double as greenhouses, industrial coffee shops that look straight out of *Architectural Digest*, and rustic bistros that transport you to a small town in Europe. But movie buffs and history nerds will certainly want to seek out Crew Collective & Café.

This ornate Old Port café opened in 2016 with a carefully pre-served view into the original splendour of Royal Bank Tower's main hall. The 22-storey, neoclassical tower dates back to 1928 when it was considered not just the tallest structure in all of Canada but the tallest building in the entire British Empire. It was also the first building in the city that was taller than the Notre-Dame Basilica.

When you step into the Crew Collective & Café, you'll feel like you're going back in time. And for some, it may feel like walking onto a Hollywood movie set. Grab one of the signature Crew Collective pop tarts and a cappuccino and take in the sights and sounds of the bustling, history-packed coffee shop.

You might notice the existing banking motifs preserved on the walls, or you might recognize the nooks and crannies from *Transformers: Rise of the Beasts* (2023) or *Moonfall* (2022), where the spectacular main hall served as a courthouse lobby. You might also recognize the interior from the political romantic comedy *Long Shot* (2019), where Seth Rogen's and Charlize Theron's characters used the lobby for a press conference.

The carefully preserved café might have drawn a lot of attention from Hollywood – it's basically a big screen star itself at this point – but even if you don't spot an A-list celebrity or director, the stunning architecture and goodies make it a place to visit in the Old Port. The Crew Collective doubles as a co-working space if you're keen to get a little work done while you refuel.

Address 360 Rue Saint-Jacques, Montreal, QC H2Y 1P5, +1 (514) 285-7095, www.crewcollectivecafe.com | **Getting there** Metro 2 to Square Victoria-OACI (Orange Line) | **Hours** Mon–Fri 8am–4pm, Sat & Sun 9am–4pm | **Tip** The Montréal–Mirabel International Airport (12300 Rue Services A-4, www.admtl.com/en/business) no longer services commercial passengers, but fans of Tom Hanks will recognize the airport from the outside as the stand-in for New York City's JFK in the film *The Terminal* (2004).

24 The *Daniel McAllister* Tug

Visit the largest preserved tugboat in Canada

The Old Port of Montreal is best known for its tourist-driven restaurants, picturesque rooftop bars, and Old World, European-inspired architecture and places of worship dotted along the Saint Lawrence coastline. Simply put – it's easy to forget that this bustling, downtown-adjacent neighbourhood once served as a shipyard and functioning port, until details and destinations like the *Daniel McAllister* tugboat cross your path.

The *Daniel McAllister* tug, originally known as *Helena*, was built in 1906 by Ontario-based Collingwood Shipyards Limited, where she worked on the Great Lakes as a steam-driven tug for the Public Works Department of Canada. The tug was eventually acquired by McAllister Towing Limited of Montreal in 1967, where she was rechristened as the *Daniel McAllister*.

She eventually retired from service in the 1980s and fell into the hands of the Musée Maritime du Quebec in Montreal. The museum committed to preserving the historic tug in order to promote the importance of maritime history in Central Canada. In collaboration with the Old Port of Montreal Corporation, the *Daniel McAllister* was completely restored to its original glory, down to its original colours, woodwork, and exact shape of each porthole and searchlight.

The century-old tugboat now resides in Montreal full-time and holds the title of the largest preserved tug in Canada at 31.18 metres (102.3 feet) long and 8.4 metres (29 feet) wide. She is the second-oldest preserved and ocean-going tug in the world behind the *Arthur Foss* in Portland, Oregon, built in 1889. The veteran boat is enjoying retirement on the edge of the Old Port. While she is not currently accepting visitors on board, she's docked a mere few feet from the boardwalk, allowing visitors and maritime enthusiasts the chance to get up close and personal with the carefully restored and preserved piece of maritime history.

Address Port de Montreal, Rue de la Commune W, Montreal, QC | Getting there Metro 2 to Square Victoria-OACI (Orange Line) | Hours Unrestricted from the outside | Tip Keep walking along the boardwalk to Bota Bota Spa-Sur-l'Eau (535 Rue de la Commune O, https://botabota.ca/en), a floating, Nordic-inspired spa and restaurant on a former commuter ferryboat dating back to the 1950s.

25 Dora Wasserman Theatre

One of the last Yiddish theatres in the world

Founded in 1958 by Ukrainian actress Dora Wasserman, this outpost of the Segal Centre for Performing Arts is one of the last remaining Yiddish theatres in the world. The legacy venue is renowned for dramatising the Jewish experience and folklore for the French- and English-speaking Montreal community, having staged over 85 Yiddish plays throughout its impressive 60-year history in the city.

The Dora Wasserman Yiddish Theatre isn't a place or a stage per se, but rather a community theatre organization dedicated to keeping the language of the Ashkenazi Jews alive. The resident theatre company can be found within the walls of the Segal Centre for Performing Arts, Montreal's premiere theatre venue and one of the most important regional theatres in Canada.

The centre is known for advocating for and representing Anglophone theatres within Montreal with plays and performances that range from a new Indigenous musical *Children of God* about the residential school system to the newest and hottest shows off-Broadway. However, the Segal Centre holds the Dora Wasserman Yiddish Theatre very close to the heart. The centre is home to one of the largest Yiddish Theatre Archives in the world which helps to draw inspiration for the seasonal Yiddish Theatre performances.

Although the Yiddish Theatre isn't as well-known as the larger Segal Centre, the audience has been steadily growing since its inception in 1958 with thousands of local and visiting theatre buffs in attendance for each seasonal performance, whether it be a long-time classic or a new original work. In fact, Dora Wasserman had received many awards over the course of her lifetime, including the Order of Canada and the Order of Quebec, for her contribution to the theatre community within the province, going beyond language and bridging the gap between the French- and English-speaking creative communities.

Address 5170 Côte-Sainte-Catherine, Montreal, QC H3W 1M7, +1 (514) 739-7944, www.segalcentre.org/en/dora-wasserman-yiddish-theatre | Getting there Metro 1 to Snowdon (Blue Line) or Metro 2 to Côte Sainte-Catherine (Orange Line); bus 129 to Côte-Sainte-Catherine/de Westbury | Hours See website for schedule | Tip The sporting pitch at Parc Van Horne (4900 Avenue Van Horne) hosts public cricket games throughout the summer and into the fall and spring, as well as regular cricket tournaments for intermediate players.

26 Dorchester Square
Picnic atop a former gravesite

Saunter along Rene Levesque between Peel and Metcalfe around noon, or really at any time on a sunny day, and you'll find dozens of downtown dwellers taking advantage of the sizable green space in the middle of the downtown core. Dorchester Square is a popular spot for outdoor picnicking and al fresco lunch breaks for the office workers in the surrounding towers. But the pretty public park has a surprisingly dark history just beneath the surface level.

Tucked among the modern skyscrapers and historic architecture dotted along the main downtown artery, Dorchester Square was first established in the 1800s, when it functioned as a mass grave as a result of cholera pandemics that ravaged the city from 1799 to 1854. It might be a jolly place for a picnic today – but there are still an estimated 70,000 bodies buried just underneath the grass and walkways.

Hundreds of Montrealers pass through the historic green space on a daily basis without giving it much thought. But have you ever wondered what the charcoal-hued crosses on the cobblestoned walkways represent? The 58 crosses scattered throughout the park represent the exact site of the former Saint-Antoine Cemetery, once the largest cemetery in the city. Many tombs were excavated in the 1860s in order to be moved to the newly opened Notre-Dame-des-Neiges cemetery in the town of Mont-Royal. The space was acquired by the city of Montreal shortly after and was converted into a public green space named after the founding of the Dominion of Canada in 1867.

The former cemetery has remained largely untouched since, and most park-goers are blissfully ignorant about what lies below. Fifty-odd bodies were exhumed in 2009 during an archeological dig within the park and were sent to the Université de Montréal for research purposes. But the city has no other plans to disturb the rest of the unfortunate souls buried below the public park.

Address 2903 Rue Peel, Montreal, QC H3B 4J5 | Getting there Metro 1 to Peel (Green Line) or Metro 2 to Bonaventure (Orange Line) | Hours Unrestricted | Tip Near the southern tip of the square, you'll find the futuristic Montréal Marriott Château Champlain (1050 Rue De La Gauchetière W, www.marriott.com), designed by Quebec architect Jean-Paul Pothier for Expo '67, with arch-shaped windows enhancing its space-inspired aesthetic.

27 __Dragon Flowers

The flower queen of the Mile End

Dragon Flowers owner Tamey Lau is a household name in the Mile End neighbourhood. Although you may not know her by name, chances are you can quickly conjure up a mental image of her storefront on Rue Bernard. The legacy florist shop is easily recognizable by its eye-catching collection of white-hued, hanging bird cages that climb from the ground floor shop entrance all the way to the top floor balcony. You'll often find tourists and influencers posing in front of the unique exterior, but it's really the interior of the shop that makes this neighbourhood flower shop so special.

Lau has been at the helm of Dragon Flowers for over three decades, having started the business after immigrating to Montreal from Hong Kong. The humble floral destination began as a way for the florist to support her young children but has grown into so much more than just a flower shop. Despite the fact that her children have since grown, Lau has no desire to stop running her beloved neighbourhood landmark.

Walking into Dragon Flowers, you'll be overcome with the fresh floral smells of course, but you'll also be taken by the kind smiles from behind the counter. The family-run flower shop is a huge proponent of spreading love and kindness to everyone who walks through the doors, and that includes flower and plant newbies who might be curious but too shy to ask how to explore the right kinds of flora for their lifestyle and light.

If you're in search of a plant that requires limited sunlight to suit the corner of your apartment, or if you're hoping to curate a fresh bouquet of flowers that goes beyond carnations and roses, you'll want to pay a visit to Lau's lair. The small but mighty flower shop is always packed with new plants to adopt and colourful flowers you've never seen anywhere else. Even if you don't come out with a new plant baby, you'll leave with a smile on your face.

Address 173 Rue Bernard W, Montreal, QC H2T 2K3, +1 (514) 559-0879, www.instagram.com/dragonflowershop | Getting there Bus 80 to Du Parc/Bernard | Hours Daily 8am–9:30pm | Tip Both Fairmount (74 Avenue Fairmount W, www.fairmountbagel.com) and St. Viateur Bagel (158 Rue Saint-Viateur W, www.stviateurbagel.com) are right around the corner, so grab a single bagel from each shop and conduct your own blind taste test.

28 Ecomuseum Zoo
Owls and foxes and bears – oh my!

Did you know you can visit endemic animals of Quebec, or animals that are found only here, in their natural habitat without having to leave the island of Montreal? The Ecomuseum Zoo in Sainte-Anne-de-Bellevue is less than a half-hour commute by car from Ville Marie, but it feels worlds away from the bustling downtown core. It's a great place to meet and learn about our natural neighbors.

Dr. John Roger Bidar was the man who founded both the Ecomuseum Zoo and the St. Lawrence Valley Natural History Society as a way to educate children and families better about the environment through hands-on learning as they experience the magic of the Quebec wilderness in person.

The family-friendly wildlife park first opened its doors in 1988 and has been showcasing Quebec wildlife in an ethical fashion ever since. Animal lovers can rest assured that it's certainly not a traditional zoo. This ethical and eco-responsible animal sanctuary is exclusively home to non-releasable animals, or those that cannot be returned to the wild due to injury or other impediments that affect their ability to survive in their natural environment. As such, the zoo's mission is to provide a safe and loving home for these animals while also promoting the conservation of wildlife and natural habitats.

The Ecomuseum Zoo is currently home to more than 115 different species of animals, including river otters, snowy owls, and bald eagles. It spreads over 11.3 hectares (28 acres) of protected land. The zoological park has also been accredited by the Canadian Association of Zoos and Aquariums (CAZA), but it didn't always have such prestigious accolades. In fact, it started out under pretty humble circumstances. You'd never know to look at it today, but the Ecomuseum Zoo was built on a wetland that had been used as a landfill in the 1960s. These days, the zoo is a true animal sanctuary and a surprisingly peaceful place to get lost in the wilderness.

Address 21125 Chemin Sainte Marie, Sainte-Anne-de-Bellevue, QC H9X 3Y7,
+1 (514) 457-9449, www.zooecomuseum.ca, info@ecomuseum.ca | Getting there By car,
take the Autoroute 40 West to Chemin Sainte-Marie in Sainte-Anne-de-Bellevue to
destination | Hours Daily 9am–5pm | Tip Down the street, iSaute Montreal (3220 Rue
Jean Yves, www.isaute.ca) a sprawling warehouse packed with rock climbing walls, massive
trampolines, foam pits, and more – an energetic kid's dream!

29__Emergence of the Chief
A striking dedication to the Kanien'kehá:ka people

Canada still has a long road ahead when it comes to recognizing and commemorating the intergenerational harm that it has caused the Indigenous community. *Emergence of the Chief* is a sculpture on the Loyola Campus at Concordia University that has been regarded as a small step toward helping the public acknowledge the Indigenous land and territories they frequent on a daily basis. The sculpture project by artist Dave McGary (1958-2013) pays homage to the Kanien'kehá:ka, or Mohawk, land that the university occupies while also serving as an open-air educational tool.

The bronze sculpture is two and a half times life-size and stands tall between the Richard J. Renaud Science Complex and the Communication Studies and Journalism Building, both built on traditional and unceded Mohawk territory. It depicts the two-row wampum belt being given to a newly elected chief by a clan mother. In Haudenosaunee law, the clan mothers choose the male candidate who becomes chief. The dark bands on the belt represent the canoe and the sailing ship, a metaphor for the relationship between First Nation peoples and European settlers.

The base of the sculpture represents the turtle shell from the Mohawk Creation Story and has been inscribed with the tribes of each of the five nations in the language of each nation, English, and French.

McGary was originally from Wyoming and worked in New Mexico for most of his life. He is considered to be a master of realism in depicting Native Americans. While the majority of his pieces are in the United States, including the White House, *Emergence of the Chief* seamlessly captures the Iroquoian heritage in bronze form.

"Creating monumental dreams is a monumental passion of mine," McGary said, from his website. "Large footprints in bronze for when I'm gone is a soothing thought. Footprints for public display to touch and feel and be emotionally attached."

Address 7141 Rue Sherbrooke W, Montreal, QC H4B 1R6, +1 (514) 848-2424 | **Getting there** Bus 51, 105, 162, 356 to Sherbrooke/West Broadway | **Hours** Unrestricted | **Tip** The Concordia Stadium and the seasonal Stinger Dome (7200 Rue Sherbrooke W, www.stingers.ca) are also located at the Loyola Campus. Catch a home game and cheer on the Concordia Stingers.

30__Eva B. Boutique
Saint Laurent's best treasure trove

"Eva B. has been here since forever!" the Saint Laurent Boulevard boutique proclaims. In actuality, the whimsical storefront and café has been providing Plateau residents with gently used, contemporary clothing and vintage finds since 1987 when founder Gabriel Croteau opened the shop with the intention of selling used books and his mother-in-law's old clothing.

The second-hand treasure trove is positioned right in the middle of an unassuming block of Saint Laurent, and if you don't know what you're looking for, well, there's a very good chance you'll walk right past it. The admittedly – and intentionally – sketchy-looking storefront is peppered with street art, graffiti, and very little signage to indicate where to enter the shop. Don't let that fool you. Once you pull open the unmarked doorway, you'll be greeted with a whole new whimsical world to discover – and friendly shopkeepers to help guide you as needed.

Strolling through Eva B. is an experience in and of itself. As you walk through the two-storey boutique, you'll feel almost as though you're traipsing through an oddball estate sale or getting lost in the studio of a very eccentric artist friend. Once your eyes adjust to the total chaos – from mannequins strung from the ceiling and chandeliers made of old doll parts, to year-round Christmas lights and old-school Halloween masks – you'll come to find that the kitsch boutique has something to offer pretty much anyone who cares to step inside.

Here, you'll score deals on vintage t-shirts, varsity jackets, fifties-era handbags and accessories. Eva B. also has an impressive curation of objects, like typewriters, old school suitcases, and a huge selection of used books and VHS movies. And once you've scored your treasure for the day the retro storefront also has a sit-down dining area with $1 shots of espresso and a decadent pastry menu.

Address 2015 Boulevard Saint-Laurent, Montreal, QC H2X 2T3, +1 (514) 849-8246, www.boutiqueevab.com, boutiqueevab@gmail.com | Getting there Metro 1 to Saint Laurent (Green Line); bus 55 to Place-des-Arts | Hours Mon–Sat 11am–7pm, Sun noon–6pm | Tip Kitsch'n Swell (4065 Boulevard Saint-Laurent, www.boutiquekitschnswell.com), a cheeky retro boutique with a massive selection of pin-up and rockabilly frocks nestled throughout the tiki-themed space.

31 Fireworks Festival
The best seat in the house is a folding chair

Signs that the summer season in Montreal is revving up include things like young adults guzzling wine and *depanneur* snacks in the park, colourful festivalgoers causing congestion on the yellow line to Parc Jean Drapeau, and a general *joie de vivre* in a city coming out of hibernation. And the most dazzling sign of all is the annual Montreal Fireworks Festival, also known as L'International des Feux Loto-Québec.

The fireworks festival hosts about eight or nine international pyrotechnicians over the weeks-long competition featuring stunning fireworks and music choreography week after week. The Montreal Fireworks Festival is the largest and most prestigious one in the world. The textured Montreal skyline and juxtaposing Saint Lawrence River serve as a gorgeous backdrop for pyrotechnic performances, which have been lighting up the skies of the city each summer for nearly four decades.

The fireworks are set off from inside the La Ronde amusement park over Dolphin Lake and are easily visible from all over the city. One of the best viewing spots in the city is on the Jacques Cartier Bridge, which stretches straight over the amusement park and offers incredible front row vantage points – for free. The bridge is completely closed for the firework festival from 8:30pm to 11:30pm, which gives onlookers plenty of space to spread out and set up their own folding chairs for the 30-minute spectacle, which is equal to about 6,000 unique and standalone fireworks!

It's estimated that about three million spectators attend the fireworks shows each year, with nearly 180,000 congregating on the Jacques-Cartier Bridge. So you'll want to try to arrive as soon as the bridge starts to close to secure a decent view. Don't forget to tune into provincial radio station Rythme FM from wherever you wind up to ensure you catch the broadcast of the accompanying "pyromusical" portion of the show.

Address 134 Jacques-Cartier Bridge, Montreal, QC H2K 4M2, +1 (450) 651-8771, www.jacquescartierchamplain.ca/en | Getting there Metro 1 to Papineau (Green Line); bus 50 to De Lorimier/René-Lévesque | Hours See website for schedule | Tip Also consider springing for reserved seats at La Ronde (22 Chemin Macdonald, www.sixflags.com/larondeen/events/linternational-des-feux), which will give you front row access to the show.

32 First Nations Garden

Indigenous culture from the ground up

The Montreal Botanical Garden was designated an official National Historic Site of Canada in 2008 for its extensive collection of diverse plant life and facilities. In fact, with its 75 hectares (190 acres) of outdoor space and greenhouses, it is considered to be one of the most important botanical gardens in the world due to its biodiversity and number of species. You'll find 22,000 different plant species – and counting – throughout the gardens!

While the Botanical Gardens are beautiful and captivating in their own right, the First Nations Garden, which opened on August 3, 2001, provides the most relevance to those looking to understand Indigenous herbs and plants. The .4-hectare (2.5-acre) gardens comprise the largest and most significant such space dedicated to the First Nations and the Inuit of Quebec.

The First Nations Garden was designed to honour and showcase the cultures of the Indigenous population of Canada. It is filled with species endemic to Quebec and various other North American regions, with over 300 different species throughout the plantings. Expect to find everything from rows of maple birch and pine trees to food and medicinal plants of the First Nations and Inuit, including sage, sweetgrass, and red cedar.

Considered to be a "crossroads of cultures," the public garden was conceptualized and created in collaboration with a committee of First Nations representatives to ensure the project properly reflects Indigenous cultures across Quebec. The stunning gardens are designed to be educational and also serve to showcase the methodology and know-how of Indigenous Peoples and their close relationships with the land. As such, the First Nations Garden also makes a point of highlighting the Indigenous activities that relate back to the plant world, from the construction of dwellings to using plants to create tools and other useful objects.

Address 4101 Rue Sherbrooke E, Montreal, QC H1X 2B2, +1 (514) 868-3000, www.espacepourlavie.ca/jardin-botanique | Getting there Metro 1 to Pie-IX (Green Line); bus 97, 139, 155, 439 to Du Mont-Royal/Pie-IX | Hours Mon–Thu 9am–9pm, Fri–Sun 9am–10pm | Tip Visit the neighbouring Japanese Garden (4101 Rue Sherbrooke E, www.espacepourlavie.ca/jardin-japonais), a serene escape from the bustle of the city complete with a koi pond, authentic Japanese art, and a daily tea ceremony in the summertime.

33 Fleming Mill

The only Anglo-Saxon mill in Quebec

There's no shortage of windmills in Eastern Canada. Drive from New Brunswick to Nova Scotia or to Prince Edward Island, and you'll lose count of the number of roadside windmills and turbines dotting the landscape. It is rare, however, to spot a windmill on the Island of Montreal. In fact, the Fleming Mill, or *Moulin Fleming*, is one of just 18 true windmills left in the entire province.

The Fleming Mill isn't the oldest windmill on the island, but its unique heritage sets it apart from its historic counterparts across Montreal. The only example of an Anglo-Saxon windmill in Quebec, the nearly 200-year-old windmill was constructed by Scotsman William Fleming in 1827 after a years-long trial with the Sulpicians, the *seigneurs* of the island of Montreal at the time.

The five-storey structure is unlike the remaining mills built in the New France architecture style. Instead, this structure is built using fieldstone and has a truncated, cone-shaped tower and cone-shaped roof. The masonry on the side of the mill was covered with additional wooden panelling to protect the integrity of the structure from the north-easterly wind.

Despite the fact that the Fleming Mill stopped being used in 1891 and the site began to deteriorate, it has become a well-loved and long-standing character in the Lasalle neighbourhood. It was registered as a Quebec heritage building in 1983 and underwent a complete restoration to reclaim its former glory.

Fast-forwarding to the present, it has admittedly seen better days, but the towering structure overlooking Boulevard LaSalle is still a majestic example of 19th-century, Anglo-Saxon-inspired, functional architecture. You can go and see the Fleming Mill from the outside at any time, and the site also offers guided tours inside the mill at the interpretation centre and a country theatre in the summer months.

Address 9675 Boulevard LaSalle, Montreal, QC H8R 2N8, +1 (514) 367-6439 | Getting there By car, take the Autoroute 20 W to Rue Saint-Patrick and Dupras Avenue to LaSalle Boulevard | Hours Unrestricted | Tip The Pointe-Claire Windmill (5 Avenue Saint-Joachim) is the oldest windmill on the island of Montreal. Dating back to the 1700s, the French design features a cylindrical stone tower and a movable roof that could be adjusted to face the wind.

34 Geordie Theatre & School

The city's leading English-language theatre

The arts and theatre scene in Montreal is astonishing. You can find surprisingly many forms of entertainment for a relatively small city. There's always something to see, watch, and hear. But finding creative, English-language community spaces within Greater Montreal can sometimes be a bit of a challenge. That's certainly not the case with Geordie Theatre and Theatre School.

The leading English-language theatre and performing arts school is quietly tucked into a side street in the Saint Henri neighbourhood. Maybe you've even passed by it a couple of times without really realizing what happens behind those doors. The multi-purpose Geordie Theatre School (GTS) works with both children and adults looking to build confidence and grow their acting craft and sense of creativity through multi-level workshops, after-school classes, and public classes.

Of course, the award-winning, professional theatre company is also well known for its productions. Geordie Theatre has been putting on performances both in Montreal and abroad for over four decades. They produce over 200 performances each season that connect with more than 40,000 young people on an annual basis. That's a lot of future creative performers!

The Theatre For Young Audiences is both captivating and inclusive, giving young English-language creatives a chance to experience what theatre can look like from the ground up. Currently helmed by professional stage actor Jimmy Blais and seasoned stage manager Kathryn Westoll, the theatre is committed to working with both emerging and professional artists from different cultural backgrounds and artistic disciplines. Their aim is to provide the community with relevant and inspiring dialogue across communities while evoking awareness of individuality and creative liberty within its youth-focused productions and professional productions alike.

Address 4700 Rue Dagenais, Suite 3, Montreal, QC H4C 1L7, +1 (514) 845-9810, www.geordie.ca | Getting there Metro 2 to Place-Saint-Henri (Orange Line); bus 36, 191 to Notre-Dame/De Courcelle | Hours See website for schedule | Tip Grab an ice cream down the street at Crèmerie Dalla Rose (4609 Rue Notre-Dame W, www.dallarose.ca), where you'll find handmade and unique, locally sourced ice cream flavours, like fresh Quebec corn and squash spice.

35 Gibbys Restaurant
Dining in a 200-year-old stable

Gibbys opened in 1969, when brothers and "original foodies" Allan and Gilbert "Gibby" Rosenberg took the leap and opened a world-class steakhouse inspired by the fine dining they had experienced while travelling the world. The restaurant specializing in surf and turf has since seated countless diners ordering chilled oysters and hearty steaks. Even in a decidedly old city like Montreal, half a century is a long time to serve a community. But the history of Gibbys goes back much farther.

Tucked into what was a 19th-century stable in the heart of the Old Port, this well-loved, local steakhouse affords guests the chance to enjoy their meals inside a carefully preserved piece of history. The entrance archway sits atop what was once the "Saint Pierre River" near the Huron settlement of Hochelaga. French explorers Jacques Cartier (1491–1557) and Samuel de Champlain (1567–1635) both visited the site.

The stable itself is just a little bit more contemporary. Present-day Gibbys occupies the former Youville Stables, or *Les écuries d'Youville.* The series of buildings was commissioned by the Sisters of Charity, known as the Grey Nuns, in the early 1800s, when horse stalls were established in the central courtyard. The nuns retained ownership of the structure until the 1960s, when the Rosenberg brothers took the historic but ramshackle property off their hands to redevelop the space into a cozy dining establishment.

These days, the former stables-turned-steakhouse retains much of the history while still offering an artful blend of Old World hospitality and contemporary appeal by way of seasonal and classic steakhouse dishes. The late Allan and Gibby credited their love of the dining experience as the magic behind what kept Gibbys running after all these years, and that *joie de vivre* is still apparent in every aspect of the unique dining destination.

Address 298 Place d'Youville, Montreal, QC H2Y 2B6, +1 (514) 282-1837, www.gibbys.com, info@gibbys.com | Getting there Metro 2 to Square Victoria-OACI (Orange Line); bus 35, 61, 75 to McGill/William | Hours Sun–Thu 5–10pm, Fri 5–10:30pm, Sat 5–11pm | Tip Take a walk past the Ancien hôpital général de Montréal (121 Rue Normand, www.patrimoine-culturel.gouv.qc.ca), a 300-year-old building that has been carefully preserved to provide an idea of what the Old Port looked like centuries ago.

36 Gibeau Orange Julep Cruise Night
Hot rods and hotdogs

The Notre Dame Basilica in Old Montreal or the Olympic Stadium in the East End might be the most recognizable structures of the Montreal skyline. But it's the Gibeau Orange Julep that truly earns the top spot as the most unique structure in the city. The giant, orange-shaped *casse-croûte* dates back to the 1930s and continues to be extremely well-loved for its poutine, pogos, hot dogs, and frothy "orange julep" beverage. Car lovers in particular enjoy the weekly "cruise night."

For the last few decades, every Wednesday from May to September brings out the best in retro cars and hot rods from all over Montreal and Greater Quebec, while giving automotive enthusiasts a chance to marvel at this casual classic car show that is best enjoyed with a hot dog or sweet and frothy beverage. The whimsical, three-storey, orange backdrop sets the stage for a rainbow-hued barrage of colourful hot rods and classic cars corralled around this Montreal institution.

All car enthusiasts are welcome to partake as long as their vehicle is pre-1980s. If you drive a modern car, or you're commuting on foot, you're still welcome to visit the Orange Julep to attend this specialty automotive meet-up. It's free for anyone interested in catching a glimpse of some of the most interesting, old-school cars in the city. But you might want to park elsewhere unless you're driving something really unique.

The weekly classic car meet-up begins around 7pm, and you'll want to stick around throughout the evening. The Orange Julep staff offers weekly contests with "best car" categories that include the Best of the Sixties, Seventies, Eighties, Best Corvette, and Most Memorable. Announced at sunset, the winner receives bragging rights, a cheeky trophy and a free Orange Julep meal.

Address 7700 Boulevard Decarie, Montreal, QC H4P 2H4, www.orangejulep.ca, +1 (514) 738 7486 | Getting there Metro 2 to Namur (Orange Line); bus 17, 115, 368, 371, 382 to Décarie/Paré | Hours Cruise Night every Wed May–Sep at dusk, shop open Sun–Thu 8pm–3am, Fri & Sat 8pm–4am | Tip About 45 minutes outside of the downtown core, you'll find Musée Gilles Villeneuve (960 Boulevard Gilles Villeneuve, www.museegillesvilleneuve.com/en), a compact museum focusing on the incredible life and accomplishments of beloved Formula 1 driver Gilles Villeneuve.

37 — The Gorgosaurus Skeleton

Who knew a dinosaur went to McGill?

Unless you're a student or alumni of McGill University, there's a good chance you've never come across this noteworthy museum tucked deep inside the campus. It looks like it might be a beautiful library or faculty building. However, when you step inside, you'll find an incredible collection of natural history artifacts unfolding in front of you.

The Redpath Museum is the oldest structure in Canada designed specifically to be a museum. It was built as a gift from sugar baron Peter Redpath in 1882 by Montreal architects A.C. Hutchison and A.D. Steele in an unusual Greek Revivalist and ornate Victorian Classicism architectural style that has retained much of its original design over its lifetime, thanks to immense conservation efforts. But as impressive as the building is, paleontology and geology enthusiasts will find the contents even more impressive.

The first thing you'll notice is the towering, full-sized Gorgosaurus libratus skeleton positioned in the middle of the atrium-like museum wing. Juxtaposed against the soaring, turquoise ceilings and ornate interior design, the replica skeleton is a sight to behold. It's thought that this specific dinosaur died as a teenager, as it's only about 70% full-grown compared to the average adults of the species. The Gorgosaurus is about two-thirds the size of its more famous cousin the Tyrannosaurus rex. It has similarly sized forearms, but its smaller size meant it could likely run faster and might have even had sharper teeth – and more of them.

Be sure to explore more of the tens of thousands of natural artifacts speckled throughout the Redpath Museum. It was first curated by some of the same people who founded the Smithsonian Institution and has thousands of fossils, bones, and other pieces of natural history ranging from fossilized Nova Scotian scallops to the skeleton of a South American anaconda.

Address 859 Rue Sherbrooke W, Montreal, QC H3A 0C4, +1 (514) 398-4861, www.mcgill.ca/redpath | **Getting there** Metro 1 to McGill (Green Line); bus 144, 360 to Des Pins/Du Docteur-Penfield | **Hours** Tue–Fri 9:30am–4:30pm | **Tip** Sitting on a park bench directly across the street is *La Leçon*, a life-sized, bronze statue of a frazzled university student by artist Cédric Loth (888 Rue Sherbrooke O). This cheeky public artwork is complete with a fruit-branded laptop, iced coffee, and fast food spilling from his lap.

38___ Grey Nuns Residence Crypt

Resting inside and beneath the Motherhouse

Hundreds of students pass daily through the halls of the Grey Nuns Residence down the street from Concordia University. The student residency is the only downtown dorm housing currently available for Concordia University students, as well as travellers looking for hostel-style accommodations come summertime when students clear out – but residents and guests might not realize they're literally sleeping above a mass grave.

The storied property was built in 1871 to serve as a motherhouse for the Sisters of Charity of Montreal, otherwise known as the Grey Nuns. Thousands of nuns called the building home. Although you'd never know it based on the stunning neoclassical and Romanesque revival architecture and effervescent undergraduate student life, the building has a tragic past buried beneath the surface.

The Grey Nuns Residence features a cafeteria, outdoor study spaces, and community rooms for students and travellers to explore and take advantage of, the basement of the residence is out of bounds for everyone except for the Grey Nun sisters. There are 276 individuals buried in the stark basement of the residence, 323 of them are nuns from the Grey Nuns congregation. The sisters were laid to rest over a century ago and were eventually supposed to be transferred to a more appropriate burial ground. But the crypt and bodies are still there to this day due to the fact that the nuns died of an unknown infectious disease.

The Mother House was designated a National Historic Site of Canada in 2011 for its spiritual and architectural history and continues to serve as a home base for students and travellers alike. Unfortunately, there are no organized tours of the site, but those looking to spend the night above the crypt are welcome to do so come summertime when the dormitory opens up to the public for summer break.

Address 1190 Rue Guy, Montreal, QC H3H 2L4, +1 (514) 848-2828, www.concordia.ca/students/housing/residences/grey-nuns.html, residenceinfo@concordia.ca | **Getting there** Metro 1 to Guy-Concordia (Green Line) or Metro 2 to Lucien-L'allier (Orange Line); bus 24, 356 to Sherbrooke/Chomedey | **Hours** Unrestricted from the outside or during summer school holidays | **Tip** The mouthwatering scent of the *lavash* flatbread being made in the entrance to the pillow-filled restaurant Avesta (2077 Rue Sainte-Catherine W, www.facebook.com/restaurant.avesta) will draw you in immediately for a homemade Turkish snack.

LA MAISON MÈRE DES SŒURS GRISES DE MONTRÉAL

Cet édifice monumental, érigé à compter de 1869, illustre avec éloquence l'ampleur de l'œuvre caritative poursuivie par les Sœurs Grises. Pendant plus de 130 ans, ce couvent a été pour les religieuses un lieu de vie collective et de prières, le centre de leurs nombreuses œuvres de bienfaisance à Montréal et la maison mère de leurs diverses missions un peu partout dans le monde. Son apparence sobre et austère d'inspiration néoclassique, son élégante chapelle néoromane, son plan rationnel et son implantation urbaine imposante en font un excellent exemple d'architecture conventuelle de la seconde moitié du XIX siècle.

MOTHER HOUSE OF THE GREY NUNS OF MONTRÉAL

Construction began in 1869 for this monumental building, which eloquently embodies the breadth of the charitable work carried out by the Grey Nuns. For more than 130 years, the convent served the sisters as a place of community life and prayer, the centre of their many benevolent works in Montréal, and the mother house for their widespread missions around the world. With its imposing presence in an urban setting, its rational plan, a plain, austere exterior inspired by the neoclassical style, and its elegant Romanesque Revival chapel, it is an excellent example of convent architecture from the second half of the 19th century.

Commission des lieux et monuments historiques du Canada et Parcs Canada

Historic Sites and Monuments Board of Canada and Parks Canada

Canadä

39 Guimard Metro Entrance

Take an afternoon trip to Paris – by public transit

Located on a relatively quiet corner at Rue Saint Jacques and Rue McGill, the "Métropolitain" metro station entrance by French architect and designer Hector Guimard (1867–1942) at Square Victoria Park will transport commuters directly to Paris – at least for a pleasant moment. A gift to the City of Montreal from the Parisian public transport operator RATP, the cast-iron, art nouveau-style archway, including the original glass light globes, was made up of parts of demolished Paris subway entrances. The orange lights have since been replaced with plastic ones for safety, but one of the originals can be spotted on display at the Montreal Museum of Fine Art, while the other was returned to the RATP.

Guimard's distinct architectural design dates back to the beginning of the Parisian metro system in 1900, when he was commissioned to create the delicate, cast-iron structures. The elaborate entrances were installed as aesthetically pleasing guideposts to the underground commuter train system and have since become an international symbol of the French capital. This Guimard metro entrance in particular was installed in Montreal in 1967, mere months after the Montreal metro first opened its train doors to commuters in October 1966, just ahead of Expo '67.

As a token of collaboration and friendship, the RATP gave the authentic Guimard entrance to the City of Montreal to commemorate the involvement of Parisian engineers in the construction of the Montreal metro system. The structure has since been completely restored and integrated into the Quartier international de Montréal as a permanent installation and piece of public art for commuters and Art Nouveau aficionados to enjoy in the open-air park. Similar Guimard-inspired replicas can be spotted around the world, but Square Victoria is the only metro station outside of Paris to host an authentic Guimard entrance.

Address 601 Rue Saint-Antoine W, Montreal, QC H3C 1E8, www.stm.info/en/about |
Getting there Metro 2 to Square Victoria-OACI (Orange Line) | Hours Unrestricted | Tip
Hop back on the metro to Berri-UQAM Station, where you'll find *Hommage aux fondateurs
de la ville de Montréal*, a stunning, multiple-storey stained glass artwork by father and son
team Pierre Gaboriau and Pierre Osterrath that tells the story of Montreal's past, present,
and future.

40 — Habitat 67
Brutalist brilliance

University students with big plans and expertly executed master's thesis projects are a dime a dozen in a city with six major universities. But Israeli Canadian Moshe Safdie set the stage for an impactful thesis when he built the visually distinct Habitat 67 residence while pursuing his master's degree at the School of Architecture at McGill University in 1967.

Habitat 67, or simply Habitat, is easily one of the most recognizable buildings on the Montreal skyline for its 354 grey-beige, cubic, concrete blocks that have become synonymous with the city. The innovative modular housing complex of 148 residences was designed to increase the quality of life for city dwellers and continues to wow even the most blasé passersby with its omnipresent appearance on the skyline. The building is well-known and heavily photographed, but locals might be surprised to learn that visitors can actually get up close and personal with the eye-catching, Brutalist structure during one of the daily guided tours.

Although it looks like an island from the shores of Old Montreal, the century-old Cité-du-Havre neighbourhood that hosts Habitat 67 is, in fact, a peninsula that was created for Expo '67. It juts out from Point Saint Charles and is easily accessible by both car and bus. When you visit the storied building complex, you'll be taken through the suspended terraces and pedestrian walkways – and you'll even get a behind-the-scenes peek into one of the 148 residential units overlooking the St. Lawrence River and the Old Port of Montreal.

The 90-minute tour runs from July to October, and all fees go toward maintaining and enhancing the architectural wonder and Montreal touchstone. Tours of the heritage complex do not run every day of the week, so you'll want to plan ahead if you're hoping to catch a glimpse of the interior bridges and walkways that make up Habitat 67.

Address 2600 Avenue Pierre-Dupuy, Montreal, QC H3C 3R6 +1 (514) 866-5971, www.habitat67.com, info@habitat67.org | Getting there By car, take the Autoroute 10 E to Chemin des Moulins, turn left on Avenue Pierre-Dupuy and follow to destination | Hours Unrestricted from the outside; see website for tour times | Tip Moshe Safdie is also the architect for the 1991 Montreal Museum of Fine Arts building (1380 Rue Sherbrooke O, www.mbam.qc.ca).

41 Haunted McTavish Monument

A moneyed mystery

There are ghost stories and then there are mysteries. The haunting of Scottish-born Simon McTavish (1750–1804) happens to fall squarely into both categories. The late McTavish was the richest man in Montreal from his work as a fur trader and chief founding partner of the North West Company. Known as the *Marquis* due to his refined taste, societal status, and unwavering generosity, McTavish's untimely death felt like a cruel twist of fate for his family and friends.

He died suddenly in 1804, when he was just 54 years old, from what was believed to be pneumonia. He left his fortune to a number of his loved ones, who turned his lavish home on Mount Royal into an opulent, walled mausoleum in his memory. Then people began reporting paranormal sightings. The late fur baron was seen dancing on the roof of his home, sledding down Mount Royal in a coffin, and peeking out of his windows at unassuming passersby.

Although the mausoleum was considered an iconic monument within the city for over a century, the site eventually crumbled. Rather than restoring it to its former glory, it was eventually destroyed and covered in rubble to prevent grave robbing and hopefully quell any further paranormal activity. But McTavish didn't let go of his glory that easily. The city tore down the residence in 1861, and during the demolition, a construction worker fell three stories and died. It's said that the ghost of Simon McTavish pushed him in retaliation for the city destroying his dream home. There were no more paranormal activity complaints after the mausoleum was gone.

Today, all that remains of the mausoleum is a small, stone marker in Monument Park. While some say the city's treatment of its most significant businessmen in the afterlife is a disgrace, many people are simply relieved his ghost has been dormant – thus far.

Address Mount Royal Park (off Rue Peel), Montreal, QC H3A 1A1, +1 (514) 486-8018 | Getting there Metro 1 to Peel (Green Line); bus 144, 360 to Des Pins/Redpath | Hours Unrestricted | Tip Make your way back down the mountain and pay a visit to the neighbouring McCord Stewart Museum (690 Rue Sherbrooke W, www.musee-mccord-stewart.ca/en), where you'll find a century-old portrait depicting the likeness of Simon McTavish by artist Donald Richings Hill.

42 The Heart from Auschwitz

Through the eyes of Montreal's survivors

It's no exaggeration to say that the Montreal Holocaust Museum is one of the most impactful yet emotionally draining public spaces in the city. The museum is intentionally curated to take visitors through a lateral timeline of life before World War II, the height of Nazi Germany, and what it looked like to rebuild after living through the death and destruction of the Holocaust, all through the eyes of Montreal-based survivors.

The Heart from Auschwitz within the walls of the Montreal Holocaust Museum is not a textbook history lesson or impersonal attempt to quantify the damages of the war but a personal look at what resistance and hope looked like when facing the unthinkable horrors of life within a concentration camp.

The Heart from Auschwitz is a small, heart-shaped, origami-like book with "F" carefully embroidered on the top of the pink-hued fabric. This artifact was gifted to Fania Fainer (née Landau) from her friend Zlatka Pitluk on December 12, 1944, a handmade token to celebrate Fainer's 20th birthday. The two Polish-Jewish prisoners were enslaved as labourers inside a munitions factory, alongside 18 of their friends, whose handwritten birthday wishes can be found within the pages of the compact birthday gift. The notes are written in French, Polish, Hebrew, and German, alongside Fainer's favourite mantra: "Freedom, freedom, freedom."

Fainer kept the gift with her for the remainder of her detention and managed to bring it with her on the horrific death march to Ravensbrück and Malchow concentration camps, despite the personal risk that it represented should it have been discovered. The heart was the only possession she had in the world when she was freed, and she cherished the tiny token for decades after the war. She would donate it to the museum in 1988, where it remains a strong symbol of strength, friendship, humanity, and resistance.

Address 5151 Chemin de la Côte-Sainte-Catherine, Montreal, QC H3W 1M6, +1 (514) 345-2605, museeholocauste.ca/en, info@museeholocauste.ca | Getting there Metro 2 to Côte Ste-Catherine (Orange Line); bus 55 to Clanranald/Dupuis | Hours Mon–Thu 10am–5pm, Fri 10am–2pm, Sun 10am–4pm | Tip Pay a visit to the Museum of Jewish Montreal (5220 Boulevard Saint-Laurent, www.museemontrealjuif.ca) to get to know the diverse culture and heritage of the city's Jewish community. It is the only museum of its kind in Canada.

43 Henri Henri Hats
The birth of the hat trick

Located on the corner of Rue Sainte Catherine and Avenue de Hotel-de-Ville in what was previously the city's Red Light District, Henri Henri Hats has become synonymous with fine headpieces and master hatmaking. The charming, old-world shop was founded as a humble family business by Honorius Henri and Jean-Maurice Lefebvre in 1932, and it continues to be a family affair, with Lefebvre's grandson Jean-Marc Lefebvre holding the reins.

While the hat shop remains one of the best spots in the city to seek out everything from high-end formal headwear to modern toques and baseball caps, it's also the birthplace of a little-known but major piece of National Hockey League history. The shop happens to be where the celebratory term "hat trick" was brought into the sport of hockey. Beginning in 1947, co-founder Jean Maurice Lefebvre rewarded every NHL player who scored three goals or more in one game, regardless of their team, with a brand new hat of their choice. And clearly the term has stuck!

Although the storied shop no longer honours the original hat trick offer, it remains one of the most fun boutiques in the city – who doesn't want to try on a zillion hats? Celebrity clients range from the Montreal Canadiens to movie stars, like John Travolta and Robert de Niro. This hat specialist stocks headwear and headpieces of all price ranges and styles, from 50-dollar berets to 1,000-dollar fedoras. Stop by, and Henri Henri's well–versed staff will help you find the hat to suit your personal style and price point.

Henri Henri is also well-stocked with hat blocks, steam machines, and other tools to help preserve and repair used and antique hats of all styles that could use a little trip to the hat spa. So you can bring in your grandfather's favourite fedora to be preserved and repaired for a new life atop your own head, or trust in your sales associate to find you a brand new cap.

Address 189 Rue Sainte-Catherine E, Montreal, QC H2X 1K8, +1 (514) 288-0109, www.henrihenri.ca/us | Getting there Metro 1 to Saint Laurent (Green Line) or Metro 2 to Champ-de-Mars (Orange Line) | Hours Daily 10am–6pm | Tip Half a block down the street, you'll find Pub Le Sainte-Élisabeth (1412 Rue Sainte-Elisabeth, www.facebook.com/PubSteElisabeth), and walk directly out onto the terrace, which is a green oasis with overgrown vines and mature trees juxtaposed against the red brick walls.

44 Holiday Inn Koi Pond
Wind down in Chinatown

The Holiday Inn Montreal Centreville Downtown at the corner of Chinatown and Old Montreal is impressive in its own right. The three-star hospitality outpost is instantly eye-catching thanks to the addition of Chinese-inspired *xieshan* pagodas that adorn the tippy-top of the downtown building. The 221 room hotel welcomes budget-conscious travellers with basic but well-appointed guest rooms and no-nonsense lobby. However, this hotel offers more than meets the eye.

Not only is the architecture inspired by neighbouring Chinatown, but this Holiday Inn is also home to the welcoming Le Lotus Bar lounge and Chez Chine restaurant. Flowing all around the lobby lounge and restaurant is a wonderful, indoor koi pond filled with a variety of colorful fish that will swim up alongside patrons enjoying house-made Chinese food, including Cantonese-style shrimp cro-quettes and braised mushrooms with vegetables and sea cucumber, or simply a quick glass of house wine or Tsingtao beer. There are several tables beneath the pagoda that extends out into the water, where you can dine even closer to the fish.

Located on the second floor of the hotel, the stunning and, quite frankly, surprising oasis with its indoor waterway comes as a much-needed moment of Zen for wayward travellers arriving from the airport. It is also a quiet spot right across from the busy convention centre and a block from Old Montreal for anyone seeking to reflect and unwind. You are welcome to relax on one of the comfortable, leather couches nearby and feel any tension melt away as you watch the orange-hued fish dart along the trickling waterways below you.

If you're not in the mood to sit and stay for a while, hotel guests and visitors can simply take a short stroll alongside the intricate waterway paths just to enjoy the majestic fish, which are traditional symbols of courage, perseverance, and bravery.

Address 999 Rue Saint-Urbain, Montreal, QC H2Z 0B4, +1 (514) 878-9888, www.ihg.com/holidayinn/hotels/us/en/montreal/yulca/hoteldetail/dining | Getting there Metro 2 to Place-d'Armes (Orange Line); bus 55, 363 to Saint-Urbain/De La Gauchetière | Hours See website for dining hours | Tip For even more stunning tropical fish, Aquarius (2347 Rue Jean-Talon E, www.aquariusweb.qc.ca) is a second-generation, family-run aquarium specialty shop that has been importing tropical fish directly from Singapore for over 60 years.

45 Indigenous Voices of Today
A powerful display of resilience

The McCord Stewart Museum on Rue Sherbrooke is one of the best resources for researching and better understanding Montreal's complex history. The public research and teaching museum first opened its doors in 1921 and continues to be the leader in the preservation and appreciation of all facets of Canadian history and the nation's greater geopolitical and cultural position in the world.

There's plenty to learn and understand within the archives of the McCord Museum, but your time is perhaps best spent exploring the exhibition *Indigenous Voices of Today: Knowledge, Trauma, Resilience.* The permanent exhibition thoughtfully showcases the often-ignored or buried history and ongoing present-day strife of Indigenous peoples in Quebec and Canada through first-person stories, curated objects, and multimedia works of art in order to provide the public with a better understanding of Indigenous philosophy, knowledge, and resilience.

The thoughtful exhibition is curated in part by over 800 members of the 11 Indigenous nations in Quebec and includes over 80 different personal stories and triumphs from each Indigenous community in the province. This experience, combined with over 100 hand-selected objects from McCord Museum's Indigenous Cultures collection, fosters a meaningful encounter for visitors that shines the spotlight on how forced assimilation has stifled or undermined countless Indigenous peoples' dreams and aspirations for generations.

The collection consists mainly of gifted possessions and artifacts that date back more than 200 years in Indigenous history, such as traditional masks and costumes, Algonquian snowshoes, Kanien'kehá:ka (or Mohawk) cradleboards, and even leisure-focused items, including a colourful Gwich'in game bag, all designed to highlight the real stories of Indigenous peoples of Quebec, past and present.

Address 690 Rue Sherbrooke W, Montreal, QC H3A 1E9, +1 (514) 861-6701, www.musee-mccord-stewart.ca/en, info@mccord-stewart.ca | Getting there Metro 1 to McGill (Green Line) | Hours Tue, Thu & Fri 10am–6pm, Wed 10am–9pm, Sat & Sun 10am–5pm | Tip Across the street at the McGill campus (845 Rue Sherbrooke W) in the summer and autumn, you'll find a quaint, one-man hot dog cart. Its location on campus works around the strict street-food vendor laws in the city to serve up sausages and veggie dogs with all the fixings.

46 Jacques de Lesseps Park
It's a bird! It's a plane!

Plane spotting has long been a popular pastime for aviation enthusiasts. But it became an even more common activity during World War II, when civilians in certain countries were encouraged to look for planes as a way to help with public security. Britain, for example, was home to the Royal Observer Corps, a civil defense organization that worked to identify and track any and all aircrafts flying within British airspace from 1925 all the way till 1995.

These days though, modern plane spotters are more likely to include travellers, families, and keen photographers in addition to aviation enthusiasts. You'll see all walks of life gathering to watch the planes coming and going at Jacques de Lesseps Park in Dorval. The green space outside of the Montréal–Pierre Elliott Trudeau International Airport was specially designed to give plane-spotting enthusiasts the best vantage point to see take-offs and arrivals.

Named after French aviator Jacques de Lesseps, the observatory park was first opened to the public in 2012 by Aéroports de Montréal (ADM) as a celebration of the airport's 70th anniversary. The park is set directly next to the runway 06R/24L, which means it grants access to a specific area where aircrafts will either be reaching full speed while taking off or flying very, very low (sometimes scarily so!) while landing at YUL.

The views from this park, designed and maintained by the airport, are considered some of the best because of its unique vantage point and its amenities. There are bleachers where you can sit and watch comfortably, a well-maintained park space, and a man-made, hilly mound designed to provide better views of the planes. There are also public washrooms and plenty of parking spaces, which means you'll often see families here setting up tents, blankets, and lawn chairs for the day, or couples out enjoying romantic picnic lunches under the aircraft-dotted skies.

Address 700 Avenue Jenkins, Dorval, QC H9P 2W6 | Getting there Bus 202, 378 to Côte-de-Liesse/Halpern | Hours Unrestricted | Tip For a more intimate experience, head further down the street to the field at the end of Jenkins. This unofficial plane-watching spot in an unmanicured field sees way fewer visitors due to its lack of amenities but offers equally good views of aircrafts coming and going.

47 Jeanne Mance Monument
The founding mother of Montreal medicine

The imposing block of buildings that separates Saint Urbain and Parc that marks the transition from downtown to the Plateau is the Hôtel-Dieu de Montréal. Most people walk by the compound without giving much thought to its story. Some may recall that it hosted a crucial vaccination clinic during the recent pandemic, but what greater relevance does this institution hold?

It turns out that the former hospital is one of the most historically relevant landmarks in the city, especially for those keen on modern medicine and the history of healthcare in Canada. The Hôtel-Dieu de Montréal, the very first hospital in the city, dates all the way back to 1645 and a pioneering woman by the name of Jeanne Mance (1606–1673).

The French nurse and settler arrived in New France in 1642 alongside the founding fathers of Montreal. She had recently discovered her passion for missionary work while on a pilgrimage to France's Champagne region. So she joined the early French colonizers with the goal of founding a hospital in Montreal similar to Canada's first hospital, the Hôtel-Dieu de Québec in Quebec City.

With the support of French Queen Anne of Austria, the wife of King Louis XIII, and the Jesuits, Mance founded, single-handedly ran, and provided care at the Hôtel-Dieu de Montréal for more than a decade before returning to France to seek financial assistance to recruit sisters of the Religieuses hospitalières de Saint-Joseph to join her medical mission in Montreal.

Today, the Hôtel-Dieu de Montréal stands as a historical reminder of what Mance did for the city and its humble healthcare beginnings. A bronze depiction of the famed nurse providing aid to an injured colonist stands as an ode to the mother of medicine. The monument was created in 1909 by Canadian sculptor Louis-Philippe Hébert to mark the 250th anniversary of the arrival of the first three hospital sisters.

Address 201 Avenue Pine W, Montreal, QC H2W 1R5, +1 (514) 849-2919, www.museedeshospitalieres.qc.ca/en | Getting there Bus 55, 363 to Saint-Urban/De Pins | Hours Unrestricted | Tip Explore inside the former hospital grounds at the Musée des hospitalières de l'Hotel Dieu de Montréal (201 Avenue Pine W), where you'll find centuries-old medical artifacts and gain a better understanding of the birth of modern medicine in Montreal.

48_John McCaffery's Grave

A not-so-touching tombstone

Most graveyards have strict rules against certain inscriptions and sentiments – no obvious profanities, for example. But the gravestone of one John Laird McCaffery managed to skirt those rules through a highly cheeky form of poetry that passes as a touching tribute, but only if you don't look closely enough.

Tucked among rows of headstones engraved with thoughtful prose and eulogies at the Notre-Dame-des-Neiges Cemetery, John Laird McCaffery's tombstone inscription would make even the most hardened of crypt keepers blush. But to see it, read the tombstone vertically starting from the left, like an acrostic poem. Then you'll see in an instant what most people miss.

So how did Mr. McCaffery end up with such a sacrilegious epitaph within an otherwise perfectly respectful graveyard? There are plenty of thoughts and theories swirling around the city, but the common consensus has to do with a dramatic, triangular lovers' quarrel that lasted into the afterlife. Rumour has it that McCaffery's wife and his mistress got together after his passing to pen this epitaph in the form of an acrostic poem that lets him know exactly how they felt about his alleged adultery, infidelity, and other wrong doings. "This guy's ex-wife and mistress came in together and ordered the stone," the engraver told the *Montreal Mirror* newspaper. "They said the message represented him. It was a thing between the three of them."

John Laird McCaffrey was born in Toronto in 1940 and died in 1995, and he became much more famous after his death than in life. His infamous tombstone has made its way onto travel blogs and YouTube channels for the shocking surprise it holds. Another story alleges that McCaffrey was a well-known practical joker in his day and that the hidden message engraved on the tombstone was of his own volition. Either way – it's certainly an ostentatious approach to an epitaph.

Address 4601 Chemin de la Côte-des-Neiges, Section C, Plot 01369, Montreal, QC H3V 1E7, +1 (514) 735-1361, www.cimetierenotredamedesneiges.ca/en | **Getting there** Bus 165 to Cimetière Notre-Dame-des-Neiges | **Hours** Mon–Sat 8am–5pm, Sun 9am–5pm | **Tip** Hike through the neighbouring trails of Mont Royal to Beaver Lake (2000 Chemin Remembrance, https://montreal.ca/en/places/parc-du-mont-royal), a perfect spot to have a lakeside picnic in the summer or to skate around the frozen rink come wintertime.

49 Largest Wooden Coaster

Soar through the air with the greatest of anxiety

Roller coasters aren't for everyone, but for the wild bunch who get their thrills from racing at rapid speeds, there's nothing like getting strapped into a hunk of metal and getting your insides tossed about. The anticipation builds as you wait in line for the thrill ride – the camaraderie of the crowd, the screeching of passengers as they *woosh* by overhead…

Tucked into the middle of Parc Jean Drapeau, La Ronde has become an easily recognizable part of the Montreal skyline. It's something to marvel as you drive across the Jacques Cartier Bridge, or a great place to spend your day getting nauseous while being launched into the sky or spun round-and-round in the teacups. This sister park to Six Flags might seem like a casual course for kids and curious adults, but La Ronde is actually home to some major superlatives when it comes to amusement park history and thrill-ride culture.

Case in point: Le Monstre. Built in 1985, Le Monstre is not just the largest wooden roller coaster in Canada, but it is also the tallest, two-track, wooden roller coaster in the world. The towering structure at the back of the park is flanked by newer and faster coasters with cutting-edge tech and eye-catching neon colours, but ask any roller coaster fiend, and they'll quickly recite a laundry list of reasons why the wooden coaster is incomparable to anything else in the park.

Le Monstre was conceptualized by Montreal-based Martin & Vleminckx and stands tall at 39.9 meters (130.9 feet), making it the second largest coaster in the park after the Goliath. The wooden structure has a top speed of 96.1 kilometres (59.7 miles) per hour, with a hard first drop, airtime hills that allow passengers to "float" due to the loosely fitted seat belts (don't worry – it's safe), and enough creaking and cracking to make you wonder if strapping yourself in was the best idea in the first place.

Address 22 Chemin Macdonald, Île Sainte-Hélène, Montreal, QC H3C 6A3, +1 (514) 397-2000, www.sixflags.com/larondeen | Getting there Metro 4 to Jean-Drapeau (Yellow Line); bus 769 to La Ronde | Hours See website for seasonal hours | Tip Pay a visit to Le Galopant while visiting La Ronde. The world's oldest galloping carousel was built in Belgium in 1885 and traveled to fairs around the world, including Expo '67. The carousel was installed permanently at La Ronde in 1967 to celebrate the park's 40th anniversary.

50 La Boutique Boreale
Thoughtful souvenirs

There's a lot of noise to sort through when shopping in the Old Port. The area today is geared toward first-time tourists and cruise ship passengers who might not have the time or desire to venture further into the city for some of the lesser known or more "authentic" Montreal experiences. But that's not at all the case with La Boutique Boreale. This curated shop gives travellers – and locals – easy access to an abundance of artwork and gifts from Canadian artists and artisans, many of which are created by Indigenous people.

La Boutique Boreale opened as an extension to Images Boréales Galerie d'Art Inuit, an art gallery that boasts the largest collection of Inuit art in all of Canada. Images Boréales focuses on fine art, with associated price points. La Boutique Boreale, on the other hand, is more accessible to all. It also allows the Boreale team to show artists who practice different mediums, such as prints, clothing, pottery, moccasins, and more. The artists receive a percentage of the sales that include their designs.

The multi-storey boutique and art gallery is not your average gift-shop. Take your time to get to know the local artists on display in the upstairs gallery, and marvel at the intricacy of the Inuit sculptures on pedestals and hanging on the exposed brick walls. Then go down to the lower level for an equally well-curated shopping experience.

La Boutique Boreale has become one of the best spots for seeking out thoughtful gifts and souvenirs that you know are locally sourced and provide ethical relationships between the gallery and the artists. It feels like an intriguing shop in a museum. The exquisite curation of Indigenous accessories and affordable artwork is a visual feast to the eyes as it is, and the boutique will also facilitate custom design requests for the artists on display if you have something special in mind.

Address 4 Rue Saint-Paul E, Montreal, QC H2Y 1G1, +1 (514) 903-1984, www.boutiqueboreale.com, info@boutiqueboreale.com | Getting there Metro 2 to Place-d'Armes (Orange Line); bus 715 to De la Commune/Saint-Jean-Baptiste | Hours Daily 10am–6pm | Tip Further into the Old Port is Marché Bonsecours (350 Rue Saint-Paul E, www.marchebonsecours.qc.ca), a century-old public market that retains much of its original charm and was even designated a National Historic Site of Canada in 1984.

51 La Sala Rossa

Vamos a bailar

La Sala Rossa is an alternative entertainment venue that holds regular poetry slams, jazz nights, and spoken word performances, and the sensational Plateau location also happens to serve decadent Spanish tapas and paella downstairs. It wasn't always a hot spot for live music and creative pursuits, though. The building that La Sala Rossa occupies first opened its doors as part of a Jewish cultural and recreation centre back in 1932.

The cultural centre and political headquarters hosted dozens of major, cross-border, public figures and politicians, including American concert artist and activist Paul Robeson and First Lady Eleanor Roosevelt, to name a few. It also hosted the Workmen's Circle in the 1940s and 1950s, a Jewish nonprofit organization that worked to foster social and economic justice while promoting Jewish culture through education, offering Yiddish classes, lectures, and secular holiday celebrations.

These days, the historic building functions a little differently. The Centro Social Español has occupied the building for more than three decades and it continues to function as a cultural centre for those of Spanish descent. However, in true Montreal fashion, look a little deeper and you'll find the building to be a melting pot of historic and present-day cultures weaving together to create something even better.

As fate would have it, La Sala Rossa, or simply "Sala" to regulars, moved into the concert hall above the Centro Social Español just over 20 years ago, when La Sala Rossa co-founder Mauro Pezzente was looking for a bigger venue to cater to a growing population of alt-culture fiends and the Centro Social Español was looking to rent out its upstairs space. The rest is history and sort of an unexpected match made in heaven; two decades of bringing together alternative and experimental musical performances upstairs and Spanish culture downstairs.

Address 4848 Boulevard St Laurent, Montreal, QC H2T 1R5, +1 (514) 844-4227, www.casadelpopolo.com/en/events/la-sala-rossa | Getting there Metro 2 to Laurier (Orange Line), then walk 10 minutes; bus 55, 363 to Saint-Laurent/Saint-Joseph | Hours See website for showtimes | Tip Step into nearby Boucle & Papier (5183 Boulevard Saint-Laurent, www.boucleetpapier.com), local paper and gifting store that stocks stunning local and handmade stationery, greeting cards, and accessories for crafting, all in a stunning, light-flooded storefront.

52 Le HonkyTonk de Lachine

Learn to line dance

Jacques Godin and Diane Girard knew they were onto something when they first opened the doors of Le HonkyTonk de Lachine in 2005. The pair originally owned a dance school known as Cowboy Rhythm, but as more and more amateur dancers of all ages showed interest in a warm and inviting spot to convene over country music – a rarity in Montreal – Le HonkyTonk felt like the natural next step.

Godin and Girard managed their dance school as well as this non-profit club for many years. With their experience in both teaching and entertaining, they drew regular crowds to the Country and Western-inspired club. Unfortunately, Girard passed away in 2014, and Godin in 2016. However, before his demise, Godin had formed a committee to keep Le HonkyTonk alive in Montreal. These days, the venue is a non-profit dance hall managed by the same group of passionate volunteers.

When you step inside Le HonkyTonk for the first time, you'll instantly feel transported to suburban Texas or Tennessee, as the Country Western ambiance is carefully thought out and looks and feels worlds away from Montreal. The crowd on any given night is wide-ranging, from revelers in their twenties to dancers in their 80s, all bonding over the melancholic ballads and Western twang of Country music old and new.

Of course, there's no pressure to jump right into line dancing immediately if you'd prefer to sit back and enjoy the atmosphere for a little while before pulling on your boots and hitting the dance floor. While Le HonkyTonk offers beginner, intermediate, and advanced dance classes four days a week, the club is also open to the public for practice on Friday nights, and Saturdays usually host a specific theme night. Plenty of people stop by to have a few drinks with friends while listening to the music and taking in the incredible spectacle of a Country Western bar in Montreal.

Address 2915 Rue Notre Dame, Lachine, QC H8S 2H4, +1 (514) 637-8899, www.honkytonklachine.com | Getting there Bus 195 to Notre-Dame/29e Avenue | Hours See website for class and events schedule | Tip Visit the Fur Trade at Lachine National Historic Site (1255 Boulevard Saint-Joseph, parcs.canada.ca/lhn-nhs/qc/lachine). The building on the banks of the Lachine Canal has been expertly cared for and provides a glimpse into what the old part of the island looked like in the 1800s.

53 Leonard Cohen Home
Where the music lived

"Seeing Leonard Cohen walking on Saint Laurent when I was 21 was enough to make me feel like I had a home," Arcade Fire front man Win Butler wrote on *McGill News* online. Sure, there are signs of Cohen (1934–2016) all over the city, from the towering mural on Rue Crescent to his gravesite at the Shaar Hashomayim cemetery. But it's his humble, gray stone apartment in the Plateau neighbourhood (overlooking Rue Marie-Anne, no less) that has the most heart and soul.

Leonard Cohen's triplex home at 28 Rue de Vallières doesn't have any obvious signage or plaques to indicate that the singer and poet once resided at the humble residence, but the subtle clues are there if you look hard enough. The residence and neighbouring Parc du Portugal became a gathering place for Montrealers mourning the loss of Cohen who died at the age of 82. The stoop and surrounding sidewalks were flooded with flowers and mementos honouring the late recording artist, while amateur musicians took turns leading the crowd through a classic Leonard Cohen setlist.

Cohen was frequently spotted in Parc du Portugal, where he would go and sit with his laptop or catch up with neighbours. And he was also known to spend time at major Plateau institutions. He'd regularly grab a smoked meat sandwich at the Main Deli Steak House, and he never said no to a classic Montreal bagel at the flagship St-Viateur Bagel or Bagels, Etc. He was regularly spotted sporting his most comfortable pair of slippers as he picked up his morning espresso or breakfast pastries.

Parc du Portugal and the humble, gray stone triplex might not make a big show of its connection to Cohen, but you'll know you're on the right path when you reach the corner of Rue Marie-Anne Est and Rue Saint Dominique. Look up to see the guerilla signage mysteriously placed on top of the city street sign that reads: "So long, Marie-Anne, and Leonard."

Address 28 Rue Vallières, Montreal, QC H2W 1C2 | Getting there Metro 2 to Mont-Royal (Orange Line), then walk 10 minutes; bus 55, 363 to Saint-Laurent/Marie-Anne | Hours Unrestricted from the outside only | Tip Grab a cocktail at the Four Seasons Hotel MARCUS Restaurant + Lounge (1440 Rue de la Montagne, www.fourseasons.com/montreal) and enjoy some of the best unobstructed views of the 22-storey Leonard Cohen Mural *Tower of Songs* created by American street portrait artist El Mac and Montreal-based Gene Pendon.

54 Liberté Commemorative Monument

What went down during the October Crisis

Autumn of 1970 was a tumultuous and terrifying time to be living in Montreal. The October Crisis refers to the rise of the Quebec separatist guerrilla group *Front de libération du Québec* (FLQ), who kidnapped the British diplomat James Cross from his residence and murdered provincial Labour Minister Pierre Laporte in the name of overthrowing the government and liberating Quebec from the rest of Canada.

The government cracked down on these guerrilla separatists as then Prime Minister Pierre Trudeau invoked the War Measures Act for the first time in postwar Canadian history. This action eventually ended the October Crisis and led to Cross' release. Laporte's body would later be found in the trunk of a car outside of the Saint-Hubert Airport.

These days, there's not a whole lot said about the October Crisis. But you may have noticed the prominent brass and metal monument outside of the Société Saint-Jean-Baptiste de Montréal building on Rue Sherbrooke. The Liberté commemorative monument isn't an ode to the labour minister or the British diplomat, but rather to the nearly 500 separatists who were arrested and detained during the invocation of the War Measures Act.

The monument was created by Quebec artist Marcel Barbeau and lists the names of each and every separatist who was imprisoned. The brass plate reads, "Here are listed, one by one, in an equal concern for recognition of their commitment in the struggle for national liberation of the Quebec people…. The coup aimed at breaking the momentum of the people has not reached its goal. Since then, Quebecers continue the struggle for independence and will continue until the final victory. History will render them justice." The discussions and debate about separatism continue today.

Address 82 Rue Sherbrooke O, Montreal, QC H2X 1X3 | **Getting there** Metro 2 to Saint Laurent (Green Line) or Metro 2 to Sherbrooke, then walk 10 minutes; bus 29, 55, 363 to Saint-Lauren/Napoléon | **Hours** Unrestricted | **Tip** Neighbouring MAI (3680 Rue Jeanne-Mance, www.m-a-i.qc.ca/en) calls itself a "strange beast" rather than a traditional art gallery. The intercultural arts centre is an artist-driven space dedicated to serving diversified audiences while promoting intercultural exchange through various art styles and disciplines.

55 Louverture Monument
A Haitian hero

The Haitian diaspora in Montreal is one of the largest in the world, thanks in part to the fact that Montreal is the Francophone capital of the Americas. That's why, on the 375th anniversary of the founding of Montreal, the Bureau de la communauté haïtienne de Montréal (BCHM) gifted the city with a a striking, life-sized, bronze bust of François-Dominique Toussaint Louverture (1743–1803), which now stands at the helm of Parc Toussaint-Louverture, just south of the Plateau.

Toussaint-Louverture is considered to be one of the founding fathers of Haiti and the only successful leader of a slave revolt in modern history. The prominent general of the Haitian Revolution liberated Saint-Domingue from French colonial rule and founded the sovereign state of Haiti in 1804. The revolution is considered a defining moment in the Western World. It's still the only uprising that resulted in the founding of a country free from slavery and led by formerly enslaved, non-white people.

The bust of the Haitian hero holds such a significant position in the greater Parc Toussaint-Louverture, a relaxing green space that is a reprieve from the bustle of downtown. It hosts a community garden in the summer and skating rink in the winter. The figurative bronze sculpture by Haitian Canadian artist Dominique Dennery depicts Louverture in middle age, looking reflective and concerned, but with a sense of great determination. The main challenge facing Dennery, though, was that, despite Louverture's heroism, no official or realistic likeness of his facial features exists. Dennery worked from paintings, coins, and sculptures to best portray Toussaint-Louverture's pensive but forward-looking stance. The remarkable statue sits atop a pedestal that's engraved with a prominent quote by Louverture, "In overthrowing me, you have cut only the trunk of the tree of liberty. It will spring up again for its roots are numerous and deep!"

Address 137 Boulevard de Maisonneuve E, Montreal, QC H2X 1J6, +1 (514) 872-0311, www.artpublicmontreal.ca | Getting there Metro 1 to Saint Laurent (Green Line) | Hours Daily 7am–11pm | Tip The first Haitian art gallery in Montreal, Galerie Passim (6797 Boulevard St Laurent, www.galeriepassim.com) is run by friends and artists Pascal and Simon and features abstract and contemporary artwork from both Haitian and international artists.

56 — Maison Antoine-Beaudry
Where historic architecture meets contemporary art

Montreal is one of the oldest cities in Canada, and so it only makes sense that you'll find an abundance of historical and landmarked buildings speckled throughout the city, from Lachine in the West to Pointe-aux-Trembles in the East. Built in 1732, Maison Antoine-Beaudry, or the Beaudry House, is one of the oldest remaining ancestral homes in Montreal and currently functions as a community centre for visiting art exhibitions and lectures.

The Beaudry House is a former farmhouse and is considered to be the oldest intact building in the Pointe-aux-Trembles neighbourhood. But unlike many heritage buildings that fall into disuse, this one is very much in use. The farmhouse sits within Marcel-Léger Park, acting as the anchor point for dozens of cultural and family activities throughout the year and particularly in the warmer months. There are regular shows and performances, an open-air cinema schedule, a wharf installed right on site to provide heritage cruises, and a river shuttle service as well.

Those looking to have a more historically focused and culturally enriching experience should also note that the summer activities give way to a lecture schedule from all kinds of experts, as well as rotating art exhibitions from local contemporary artists and historic artworks throughout the rest of the year.

Although the cultural activities at the Maison Antoine-Beaudry take place mostly during the summer months, it's always open for appreciation from the outside. The home is considered to be an excellent representation of a French-inspired rural house that has been adapted to suit the harsh Quebec winters. The square-shaped stone masonry and gable roof are unique to the time period. Due to urbanization, the Beaudry house comes as a rare witness to the 1700s, as most of the buildings from this time period in Pointe-aux-Trembles have disappeared over the years.

Address 14678 Rue Notre-Dame E, Montreal, QC H1A 1W1, +1 (514) 872-2264, https://montreal.ca/en/places/maison-antoine-beaudry | Getting there Bus 189, 362, 410, 487 to Notre-Dame/Antoine-Bazinet | Hours See website for seasonal hours | Tip The sweet little Plage de l'Est (16240 Rue Bureau), located on the easternmost point of the island, offers a rocky coastline with incredible views of the Saint Lawrence and Prairies waterways, which look more like an oceanfront beach than a convergence of rivers.

57 Marché aux Puces Métropolitain

Hot commodity of oddities

Montreal might have relatively strict rules and regulations when it comes to street-side vendors and food stalls, but if you're willing to look inward, you'll find a pretty decent selection of secondhand oddities and budget-friendly essentials. Marché aux Puces Métropolitain in the east end of the city boasts over 700 vendors and is considered to be the largest flea market not just in Montreal but in all of Canada. The sprawling venue has something for every kind of shopper. With a little scavenging, you'll find everything from antiques and collectables to clothing and home goods.

The Saint-Léonard institution was made for a rainy day, with hundreds of thousands of items to be discovered and endless forms of entertainment to explore. It might sound a little overwhelming at first, but the colour-coded kiosks were made for shoppers to find everything they're looking for with ease, relatively speaking. You'll want to refer to the colour guidelines before diving in or skip it altogether and have fun getting a little lost in the chaos.

In the arcade section of the flea market, you'll find dozens of neon-hued arcade games, ranging from racing games to immersive, first-person action games. There's also an entire section dedicated to RC (radio-controlled) car racing and a golf simulator for those yearning to get out on the green.

The sprawling complex would take hours to consume from start to finish, and that's going to take a bit of fuel. Thankfully, you'll also find endless food and drink options in the massive foot court, including everything from Italian comfort food to Armenian and Lebanese dishes. There are also plenty of snack stands to provide a little sugar. Keep an eye out for kiosks serving up popcorn and cotton candy, miniature donuts, and ice cream.

Address 6245 Boulevard Métropolitain E, Saint-Léonard, QC H1P 1X7, +1 (514) 955-8989, www.marcheauxpucesmetropolitain.ca | Getting there Bus 55, 141, or 193 to Langelier/Jarry | Hours Thu & Fri 10am–6pm, Sat & Sun 10am–5pm | Tip Café Milano Montréal (5188 Rue Jarry E, www.cafemilano.ca) is open 24/7 for your caffeine fix. The East End institution is said to serve the best cannoli in the city, but many customers are quite fond of the decadent Beyond Meat sandwich here.

58__Marché Ghanacan

A pillar of the Ghanaian community

The Park Extension, or Park Ex, neighbourhood is a veritable melting pot of cultures and flavours. Getting off the Blue Line at Parc Station, you're instantly enveloped in the warming scents of Haitian and Indian spices, and following your nose will almost always lead you to where your mouth wants to be going. In fact, Park Extension is considered one of Canada's most ethnically diverse neighbourhoods. It used to be mainly an Italian and Greek borough in the 1960s and 70s, but for the past few decades, the neighbourhood has become home to new immigrants from all over the world, particularly those of South Asian, African, Haitian, and Ecuadorian descent.

It's nearly impossible to visit this multicultural and multigenerational neighbourhood and not stop for a bite to eat. But if you're hoping to collect the ingredients and make your own savoury meal at home, you'll want to pay a visit to Marché Ghanacan on Avenue Ogilvy. This compact yet well-appointed grocery store specializes in African and Caribbean ingredients and flavours with hundreds of imported products and fresh food that aren't easy to find elsewhere in the city, like fresh goat meat.

The 20-year-old grocery store is considered a pillar of the Ghanaian community in Montreal and goes above and beyond what you'd expect from a fruit market or butcher. The guiding ethos behind Marché Ghanacan is that everybody should be set up to succeed when it comes to cooking, whether that's traditional African dishes or North American recipes with a kick.

Once inside, you won't have to search too much for hard-to-find ingredients or get lost trying to score the best cuts of meat or fresh vegetables for your recipe, whether you're looking for tips on how to make the best *fufu* and *egusi*. This community grocery store goes out of its way to make cooking and shopping an inclusive experience for all.

Address 549 Avenue Ogilvy, Montreal, QC H3N 1M9, +1 (514) 278-6987, www.marcheghanacan.ca | **Getting there** Metro 1 to Parc (Blue Line); bus 80, 480 to Ogilvy/Querbes | **Hours** Mon–Sat 10:15am–9pm, Sun 10:15am–8pm | **Tip** Nearby Ram Sweet Shop (1016 Rue Jean-Talon W, www.facebook.com/indiansweetmontreal) is a charming, family-run dessert counter that boasts every kind of Indian sweet and savoury snacks you can imagine – and they're all priced at a dollar or two.

59 Marché Maisonneuve
The little public market that could

It's not the oldest or biggest public market in the city – that's Marché de Lachine and Marché Jean-Talon, respectively. But Marché Maisonneuve in what is now the Mercier-Hochelaga-Maisonneuve neighbourhood has arguably garnered the most public support and community love out of the public market network in Montreal. That's saying a lot for a city that loves its farmers' markets wholeheartedly.

Marché Maisonneuve first opened its doors to the public in 1912 and was originally designed and conceptualized by architect Marius Dufresne (1883–1945). The market has been through a lot since then. The market closed completely in the 1960s and eventually reopened in the 1980s, thanks to pleas from local residents.

It's now housed next to the original Beaux-Arts-style structure in a more modern building to accommodate the dozens of butchers, fishmongers, and farmers that feed what is now one of the buzziest neighbourhoods in the city. But this storied market still retains much of its original charm, thanks to the century-old architecture that dots the space, as well as the abundance of local shoppers milling about the market at any time of the week. You'll especially enjoy a visit on the weekend if you really want to get the feel of the neighbourhood.

Plan for enough time to shop for fresh produce and Quebecois cheeses and meats, and also to admire the atmosphere outside of the market as well. You'll find *La Fermière*, the fountain in the middle of the market square, to be one of the best spots to meet friends or stop and sample your gourmet haul. The monument by artist Alfred Laliberté (1877–1953) depicts a 17th-century, female farmer and was first conceptualized as a nod to local agriculture and the "sacred soil" that marked Quebecois art at the time. It's now the landmark of the Marché Maisonneuve and a testament to how much market culture means to the city.

Address 4445 Rue Ontario E, Montreal, QC H1V 3V3, +1 (514) 937-7754, www.marchespublics-mtl.com | Getting there Metro 1 to Pie-IX or Viau (Green Line); bus 125 to Ontario/William-David | Hours Mon–Sat 9am–6pm, Sun 9am–5pm | Tip There's nothing like the comforting presence of plants to evoke creativity and relaxation, so head to Leaves House (1800 Avenue McGill College RDC-A, www.leaveshouse.com) for a cappuccino and a sweet treat, and leave with one of the dozens of exotic plants that dot the café.

60 Maude Abbott Medical Museum

A museum with a warning label

Museums that come with a warning label mean business, and the Maude Abbott Medical Museum isn't joking when it says it might be disturbing to some visitors. The McGill University muscum offers a collection of medical materials that date back to the early 19th century, documenting the study and practice of medicine at the university and the medical industry in general.

The Maude Abbott Medical Museum, named for one of Canada's earliest female medical school graduates and one of the first women to obtain a BA from McGill, is not for the faint of heart. But that shouldn't deter you from visiting if you have any interest in human biology and medical advancements. In fact, you may feel like it's actually a privilege to have the chance to see the number of artifacts on display for public consumption.

Tucked deep inside the Strathcona Anatomy & Dentistry Building, this compact space is surprisingly jam-packed with hundreds of historical, medical artifacts and modern-day equipment, ranging from the intriguing to the downright creepy. Be prepared to find real human specimens too, including pathologic abnormalities that will make your skin crawl. Peruse the collection of healthcare stamps and postcards from Montreal hospitals that date from the 1880s to the 1960s. There are plenty more oddities and interesting medical devices designed to educate and enlighten you, but be prepared to be a bit disturbed as well.

Note that alongside its permanent and temporary exhibits that are open during the daytime, the Maude Abbott Medical Museum also offers regular presentations and events geared toward the medical-minded community come nighttime. Doctor-hosted "night at the museum" fundraisers and even medical-focused poetry nights and dance shows are regular occurrences.

Address 3640 Rue University, Room 2/38E, Montreal, QC H3A 0C7, www.mcgill.ca/medicalmuseum, medicalmuseum.med@mcgill.ca | Getting there Metro 1 to McGill (Green Line) | Hours Tue–Fri 1–5pm or by appointment | Tip The Osler Library of the History of Medicine (3655 Promenade Sir-William-Osler, www.mcgill.ca) opened in 1929 and houses over 100,000 rare and historical medical books. It is currently regarded as one of the largest and most valuable libraries of its kind in North America.

61 Ministry of Cricket

Gym class, all grown up

It's not uncommon for colleagues and friends to fall into the same kind of team-building or catch-up routine, especially in Montreal. More often than not, it's going to be some form of the *cinq à sept*. A few hours of drinking, maybe some bar snacks or small dishes to share, and surface-level conversation set over the bustle of a wine bar or live music at the pub. The Ministry of Cricket & Other Homeless Sports believes there has to be a better way to connect with adult friends. But don't worry – you can still have a few beers. And you're guaranteed to have more fun than you've had in a while.

Walking into the recreational centre in the Ahuntsic neighbourhood, you'll likely be struck by an instant sense of nostalgia for your elementary school gym class, and that's kind of the whole point. The Ministry of Cricket is essentially made up of generously sized indoor AstroTurf fields divided by netted curtains to create semi-private fields for groups of friends and colleagues to let out their inner elementary school kid, and also for actual elementary school kids to run wild. Meanwhile, the upstairs mezzanine overlooks the entire arena, allowing for adult beverage breaks while also giving parents a bird's eye view of the goings-on below.

Your cast of characters will choose between a handful of "homeless sports," which in this case boils down to the weird, quirky, or unusual team sports that don't get the glory of mainstream sports like hockey or basketball. You could opt for the namesake cricket, but there's room to fall into the rabbit hole of weird and wonderful sports if you really wanted to. The Ministry of Cricket boasts hilarious and social media-friendly bubble soccer, Nerf Wars, extreme archery, and even medieval battles (complete with foam swords and shields) and real-life Quidditch with muggle-friendly quaffles, bludgers, a golden snitch, and, you guessed it, broomsticks between each player's legs.

Address 1301 Rue Mazurette, Montreal, QC H4N 1G8, +1 (514) 245-3540, www.ministryofcricket.ca | **Getting there** Bus 54, 179, 365 to De l'Acadie/Chabanel | **Hours** Mon–Fri 1–11pm, Sat & Sun 10am–11pm | **Tip** Head to Saputo Stadium (4750 Rue Sherbrooke E, en.cfmontreal.com/stadium/stade-saputo) at Olympic Park, the current home of CF Montréal Major League Soccer team, and catch a home game for less than the price of a round of beer at the Bell Centre.

62 Minuit Dix Tattoo Shop

A queer-owned ink institution

Tattoo studios haven't always felt welcoming or inclusive to any-one other than tough-mugged, cis-gender men. It's still not always a guarantee that walking into a tattoo shop automatically means you're entering into a safe space for creative exploration and self-expression. But everyone is welcome at Minuit Dix.

This Mile End studio is the first openly queer-owned tattoo shop, whose team is exclusively made up of women who identify as women or non-binary people. Most of them also identify as belonging to the LGBTQIA+ community. The studio opened its doors in 2017 at a time when there weren't any others quite like it.

"Minuit Dix helped create this wonderful community of artists," explains owner Muriel de Mai. "Many female and/or queer artists have since been inspired to create their own space and get out of the traditional model of the tattoo studio, which was primarily gatekept by straight white men."

"We openly oppose and reject fatphobia, transphobia, ageism, rac-ism, and anything that undermines respect for any person," adds de Mai. "Our goal is to maintain a space that is comfortable and wel-coming to everyone!" And that very ethos plays out as soon as you walk into the vibrant space. Minuit Dix is bright and airy, which goes against the typical visions you might conjure up when picturing a tat-too studio. The space overflows with plants, and there's always some cool tune playing in the background.

The private studio operates on an appointment-only basis, which means there's no reception area for walk-ins. The artists that make up Minuit Dix are independent and manage their own schedules and bookings. Still, the studio regularly organizes flash day events, pop-up shops, and exhibitions and fundraisers for causes near and dear to the artists, so there are plenty of chances to experience the good vibes of this trail-blazing creative community.

Address 5555 Avenue de Gaspé, No. 202, Montreal, QC H2T 2A3, www.minuitdixtattoo.ca, info@minuitdixtattoo.com | **Getting there** Metro 2 to Rosemont (Orange Line); bus 13, 25, 31 to Rosemont | **Hours** Contact individual tattoo artists for appointment | **Tip** Around the corner is Annex Vintage (5364 Boulevard Saint Laurent, www.annexvintage.com), a very well-curated mix of locally made gifts, prints, and jewelry, as well as decidedly cool vintage and secondhand clothing mainly from the '90s.

63 Montreal Aviation Museum

Look up!

There's something elusive and magical about aviation history. Can you imagine being among the first to risk strapping yourself into what was essentially an experimental tin can? Historic and present-day aviation seems a bit like the bumblebee flight myth. According to the theory of aerodynamics, chunky little bumblebees shouldn't be able to fly due to their size and weight, and yet, inexplicably, they do.

Of course, the dynamics of contemporary flight are much better understood today. Airplane wings are designed to manage the air moving across them, creating a force that lifts the plane into the air or helps it gently descend. But it's still fun to marvel at the magic of flight. The Montreal Aviation Museum in Sainte-Anne-de-Bellevue is a must-visit for aviation nerds, or anybody who feels a sense of wonder while watching an airplane soar overhead.

The late Godfrey Stewart Pasmore founded the non-profit museum in 1998. His goal was to preserve the rich aviation heritage with a distinctly Quebec eye, and the collection has been carefully maintained and built upon by volunteers and aviation experts ever since. The museum is the only one of its kind in Quebec, placing emphasis not just on preservation but on education as well. Tucked into the historical Old Stone Barn on the Macdonald Campus of McGill University, the hands-on and family-friendly museum offers something for every kind of learner interested in both civil and military aviation.

Stepping into the barn-turned-museum, you'll find a collection of fully intact and historically significant aircrafts, including a Canadair CF-104 Starfighter and a Noorduyn Norseman, as well as artifacts, and memorabilia. There's even a series of restoration and construction workshops during which you can get up close and personal with the engineering side of aviation in the company of experts.

Address C375+55 Chemin Lakeshore, Sainte-Anne-de-Bellevue, QC H9X 3V9, +1 (514) 398-7948, www.mam.quebec/discover-our-museum-2, info@mam.quebec | Getting there By car, take the Autoroute 20 W to Boulevard des Anciens-Combattants, follow to destination | Hours See website for seasonal hours | Tip While in Sainte-Anne-de-Bellevue, pay a visit to Paddle Mac (21300 Rue Lakeshore, www.paddlemac.com), a family-friendly boat club offering paddle board and kayak rentals, as well as private lessons on the water.

64 Montreal Insectarium
Pretty in pink

Traipsing through rooms of free-roaming and partly confined insects and arthropods might not seem like fun for a lot of people. In fact, it's kind of the opposite. But the experience of spending time among thousands of different living and breathing species from around the world can actually have a profound effect on you – if you let it.

The Montreal Insectarium by Espace pour la Vie is a treasure hunt in and of itself, with over 3,000 different species of creatures on display for visitors to meet up close and personal at this live insect zoo. The museum was founded in 1990 by entomologist Georges Brossard (1940–2019) and maintains its reputation as one of the largest bug-focused museums in North America, thanks to its network of experiences that range from cozy, multisensory circuits to a "living kingdom" greenhouse where bugs really do fly free in their own controlled ecosystem.

Visitors can spot over 180 different butterfly species and approximately 150 different plant species as well here. But it's the elusive orchid praying mantis that will leave the greatest impression. The stunning, powder-pink-hued insect comes from Southeast Asian tropical rainforests, where it rests camouflaged on orchids to conceal itself from potential predators and to lure prey, such as bees and even butterflies, all thanks to its floral-like body shape and pastel colouring.

The orchid praying mantis is hard to spot in its natural habitat. So, although its living space is well replicated in the Tête-à-Tête section of the Insectarium, the exhibit is also designed to allow visitors to have a good look at these creatures. This section of "get-togethers" is displayed at eye level, with direct views inside the display unit of each insect. Visitors can study the physical characteristics and behaviours of this unique praying mantis and other insects too.

Address 4581 Rue Sherbrooke E, Montreal, QC H1X 2B2, +1 (514) 868-3000, www.espacepourlavie.ca/en/insectarium | Getting there Metro 1 to Pie-IX or Viau (Green Line); bus 185, 364 to Sherbrooke/No 4750 or 4751 | Hours Tue–Sun 9am–5pm | Tip Walk straight to the green at the Montreal Municipal Golf Course (4235 Rue Viau, https://montreal.ca/en/places/golf-municipal-de-montreal), a public, nine-hole golf course and driving range right in the middle of the city.

65 Montreal's Birthplace

The origins of a metropolis

What would you say is the most *Montréalaise* part of Montreal? Some might say it's the wood-fired ovens at Saint Viateur or Fairmount Bagel in the Mile End. Others might argue for the colourful architecture dotted throughout the Plateau neighbourhood. Mount Royal Park, Montreal's favorite "mountain," is a pretty decent contender too. But none of these icons can encapsulate the origins of the city quite like the exact spot where it was born.

Montreal's Birthplace is the official swathe of land that marks the location where Paul de Chomedey de Maisonneuve (1612–1676) laid the foundation of what is now known as Montreal. It's not a grand affair or particularly noteworthy landmark. In fact, you've probably already walked by it without giving it much thought, as this auspicious location is commemorated simply with a humble plaque located between Rue de la Commune W and Place D'Youville. It was here on May 18, 1642 that Maisonneuve officially founded Ville-Marie, which would become Montreal, and he would be its first governor. It must be noted, though, that the surrounding land had already been known and inhabited by Indigenous peoples for centuries.

The site also rests on the remains of Fort Ville-Marie, otherwise known as Fort Maisonneuve, which Paul de Chomedey de Maisonneuve had built in 1645 due to the ongoing conflicts between the French settlers and the Iroquois people.

The landmark, albeit small and rather insignificant looking at first glance, was officially designated as a National Historic Site of Canada in 1924 due to its significance as the official birthplace of Montreal, and Paul de Chomedey de Maisonneuve was recognized as a National Historic Person of Canada. The designation also recognized the very place that would expand from this pinpoint of a birthplace and eventually transform into one of Canada's most bustling metropolitan areas.

Address 214 Place d'Youville, Montreal, QC H2Y 2B4 | Getting there Metro 2 to Place-d'Armes (Orange Line); bus 715 to De La Commune/De Callière | Hours Unrestricted | Tip Walk for 10 minutes along the Old Port boardwalk to the Clock Tower (1 Rue Quai de l'Horloge). Built between 1912–1922, this structure memorializes sailors lost at sea.

CANADA

AUX ORIGINES DE MONTRÉAL
THE ORIGINS OF MONTRÉAL

C'est ici que le sieur de Maisonneuve fonda Montréal en mai 1642. Situé au confluent du Saint-Laurent et de l'ancienne petite rivière Saint-Pierre, l'endroit était bien connu des Autochtones qui s'y rassemblaient depuis des siècles, de même que sur le site de l'actuelle place Royale. Dès leur arrivée, les Français construisirent le fort Ville-Marie. Vers 1688, le gouverneur de Montréal, Louis-Hector de Callière, obtint une partie du terrain et y érigea sa résidence, d'où le nom de pointe à Callière. Ce lieu qui vit naître Montréal fut aussi témoin de sa transformation en l'une des grandes métropoles du Canada.

Here, in May of 1642, <u>sieur</u> de Maisonneuve founded Montréal. Located at the junction of the St. Lawrence River and the now-disappeared <u>Petite rivière Saint-Pierre</u>, this area was well known to Native peoples who for centuries met here and on the present site of Place Royale. The French built Fort Ville-Marie upon their arrival. Around 1688, Montréal's governor, Louis-Hector de Callière, acquired a portion of the area and built his residence, hence the name Pointe à Callière. This site which gave birth to Montréal also witnessed its transformation into one of Canada's great metropolitan centres.

Commission des lieux et monuments historiques du Canada
Historic Sites and Monuments Board of Canada

Gouvernement du Canada · Government of Canada   ©1997

66 Montreal Irish Memorial

The world's oldest Irish Famine memorial

Established in honour of the thousands of Irish immigrants who fled the Great Famine but ultimately passed away upon making it to Canada, the Montreal Irish Memorial, or Irish Commemorative Stone, is the world's oldest memorial to the devastating famine. Dating back to 1859, the monument is believed to be the headstone atop a 6,000-person mass grave.

Although the famine caused mass emigration to Canada of people in search of a better life, the long, agonizing trip across the Atlantic Ocean was no small feat. Thousands of Irish men and women arrived weakened by malnutrition and fatigue from the multi-week crossing and prior hunger, and many fell victim to what was known as "ship fever." The Sisters of Charity of Montreal, or the Grey Nuns, did everything they could to accommodate the ill and weakened immigrants, but thousands succumbed to the illness and were buried on the shores of the Saint Lawrence River.

The Irish Commemorative Stone was laid on top of the grave a decade later, when construction workers discovered the remains while excavating the area for the construction of the Victoria Bridge. Poetic and practical, the city of Montreal used a large stone taken from the riverbed and engraved it with the words, "To preserve from desecration the remains of 6,000 immigrants who died of ship fever A.D. 1847-8. This stone is erected by the workmen of Messrs Peto, Brassey & Betts, employed in the construction of the Victoria Bridge, A.D. 1859."

The 30-tonne rock has blackened with pollution and time, but is still a touchstone in Irish Canadian culture. Thousands of Irish descendants visit the monument to pay respects to the lost immigrants each year. In fact, the streets and urban development that surround the monument have expanded and shifted over time, having been intentionally redesigned to give the stone a more prominent placement at the base of the bridge.

PRESERVE FROM DESECRATION
THE REMAINS OF 6000 IMMIGRANTS
WHO DIED OF SHIP FEVER
A.D. 1847-8

THIS STONE
IS ERECTED BY THE WORKMEN
OF
MESSRS PETO, BRASSEY & BETTS,
EMPLOYED IN THE CONSTRUCTION
OF THE
VICTORIA BRIDGE
A.D. 1859

Address Rue Bridge, Montreal, QC H3K 1X8, +1 (514) 949-2710, www.montrealirishmonument.com | **Getting there** Bus 107 to Wellington/Bridge, then walk 12 minutes | **Hours** Unrestricted | **Tip** Head to Siamsa Montreal School of Irish Music (4873 Avenue Westmount, www.siamsa.org/en) for a lesson in traditional Irish folk music, or pop by to check out one of the regular Ceili social dances. All levels are welcome.

67 Montreal Signs Project
Illuminating local heritage

Montreal is in a constant state of flux with evolving bylaws, monumental city planning projects, and the shifting identities of neighbourhoods. According to Dr. Matt Soar in Concordia University's Department of Communication Studies, these changes are inevitably signalled through the sudden removal of eye-catching commercial signs, many familiar enough to matter to Montrealers.

The Montreal Signs Project grew out of Soar's own research initiatives, which focused on high-rise signs and hypercommercialism and the idea that there are too many advertising messages surrounding us. He tracked down discarded signs from around the city that were in danger of being lost forever. Soar "floated the idea" of putting them on permanent display on the walls in his department. Technically, no one said "no." He launched the MSP in 2010, with over fifty signs – and counting.

The signs on display are always changing and vary widely in terms of materials and design. But they all have one thing in common. Each sign is reminiscent of a Montreal of days gone by, with logos and designs easily recognizable to locals. The Monkland Tavern sign, for example, is one of Soar's favourites right now. It's not just a well-loved neighbourhood address but also an example of lovely script letters reminiscent of eccentric handwriting. The hand-painted lettering on the Belle Province Meat Co. and Wong Wing Foods signs has to be seen close-up to be appreciated, while the Steinberg supermarket logo highlights mid-century modern graphic design.

There are 25 signs from the current collection on permanent display in the CJ building on Concordia's Loyola campus, which is generally accessible to the public (just be respectful of teaching and research activities in the building). That said, some things are much better experienced on guided tours, which Soar is happy to provide by prior arrangement.

Address 7141 Rue Sherbrooke O, Montreal, QC H4B 1R6, www.montrealsignsproject.ca |
Getting there Bus 51, 105, 162, 356 to Sherbrooke/West Broadway | Hours See website
to book a guided tour | Tip Set within the walls of a former art deco public bathhouse,
the Écomusée du Fier Monde (2050 Rue Atateken, www.ecomusee.qc.ca) offers insights
into the industrial and working-class people of Centre-Sud, one of Montreal's oldest
neighbourhoods.

68 Montreal Stock Exchange
Buy low, sell high

The Montreal Stock Exchange is credited as the very first exchange in Canada when it started informally at the Exchange Coffee House in the Old Port in 1832. The initiative was spearheaded by Scottish-born banker and stockbroker Lorn MacDougall, who, along with his brothers Hartland St. Clair MacDougall and George Campbell MacDougall, helped take the Montreal Stock Exchange into a work of architecture much more suited for the up-and-coming financial centre of the country.

By 1903, the Montreal Stock Exchange commissioned a brand new building to be constructed just down the road. New York's iconic Exchange Building was just being erected, and Montreal contracted the same architect to design a similarly grandiose centre of trade up North. American architect George B. Post was known for his Beaux-Art style and is still credited as one of the masters of modern American architecture and playing a huge role in the birth of the first modern skyscrapers.

Unfortunately, the reputation of the new stock exchange building didn't have the same lasting power as the New York Stock Exchange. The Montreal Stock Exchange was deeply affected by the crash of 1929 and was eventually bypassed by Toronto as the leading exchange in Canada. Montreal's exchange was also seen as a representation of Anglo-Canadian power, which incited the separatist group Front de libération du Québec to detonate a bomb within the building's walls, injuring nearly 30 people and blowing out the northeast wall.

Not all was lost though. The Beaux-Arts brother to the NYSE still stands today as the Centaur Theatre, hosting the main and one of the only English-language theatre companies in the city. The performing-arts group purchased the building in 1974 and invested millions into renovating and preserving the historic property. It's now considered to be the centre of the Montreal artistic community.

Address 453 Rue Saint Francois Xavier, Montreal, QC H2Y 2T1 | **Getting there** Metro 2 to Place-d'Armes (Orange Line) | **Hours** Unrestricted from the outside only | **Tip** The Bank of Montreal Museum (129 Rue Saint-Jacques, www.ourheritagebmo.com/ museum) is located in the oldest bank building in the city and provides an intimate look at the financial history of Montreal, including actual tellers' stations from the 1800s.

69 Mordecai Richler's Residence
The pearl of the Golden Square Mile

The Le Château Apartments in the Golden Square Mile offer layers upon layers of historic significance and elegance waiting to be peeled back. The 136-apartment residence on Sherbrooke Ouest was commissioned by Pamphile Réal Du Trembla, owner of *La Presse* newspaper, and was erected in 1926. Built by Montreal architecture firm Ross & MacDonald in the Châteauesque style, the building shares ties to the Grand Railway Hotels across Canada and was indirectly inspired by the Plaza Hotel in New York City. It features Tyndall limestone from Garson, Manitoba, and you can find a series of fossils within the limestone of the façade that date beyond the last ice age when Manitoba was underneath the sea.

Although the property's claim to fame lies within its architectural relevance in Canada and its position in the heart of the Golden Square Mile, many famous residents over the last century have had their *pieds-à-terre* here. The most famous was author and essayist Mordecai Richler, who lived in Le Château for more than 20 years. Richler spent his time here writing and editing during the day. By night, or when the writing was slow, he would sneak across the street to the Ritz-Carlton or down the road to Grumpy's or Ziggy's to punctuate the end of the workday with a stiff drink and a round of conversation with fellow Anglophone locals.

Richler also put the Château and the Golden Square Mile neighbourhood on the international stage posthumously when the film adaptation of his novel *Barney's Version* was shot in the residence and courtyard in 2010. The courtyard is reserved for guests, but you can still catch a glimpse of the limestone façade and interior fountain from the sidewalk on Rue Sherbrooke or from the Camillien-Houde Lookout on Mont-Royal.

Address 1321 Rue Sherbrooke O, Montreal, QC H3G 1J4 | **Getting there** Metro 1 to Peel (Green Line); bus 715 to Saint-Laurent/De La Commune | **Hours** Unrestricted from the outside only | **Tip** Directly across the street, you'll find the former Holt Renfrew flagship store (1300 Rue Sherbrooke W), which now serves as a multi-purpose office building. Also by Ross & MacDonald, the Art Deco structure was named "one of the most modernly and attractively appointed retail establishments on this continent" in 1937.

70 Morgan Arboretum

Go forest bathing

Montreal is well-known for its stunning architecture, world-renowned restaurants, and wine bars, and plenty of other cosmopolitan haunts and must-sees within its city limits. But you'd be doing yourself a disservice to skip over one of the city's best places to wind down after a long day, the Morgan Arboretum.

There are plenty of science-backed studies and research that tout the benefits of "forest bathing," or spending time among the trees, as a form of free therapy. After a trip to this university-managed forest reserve, you will have a clear understanding of just how powerful the experience of simply being in the woods can be.

The Morgan Arboretum covers an ample, 245-hectare (642-acre) area on the McGill University's Macdonald Campus just outside of the city on the western edge of the island. It has been a staple in research and recreation since it first opened in 1945. Although the university utilizes this stunning forest reserve for teaching and scientific purposes, it's also open to the public for a small fee. Visitors can enjoy the intricate paths year-round for hiking, snowshoeing, or cross-country skiing. There are more than 40 native species of trees on the grounds, including the American beech, sugar maple, butternut, bitternut hickory, and black cherry trees, to name a few. The mixed-use woodland area is also home to an impressive 170 species of birds, 15 species of reptiles, and over 30 different species of mammals.

The arboretum also recognizes the city of Montreal's affinity for summertime and outdoor leisure. In that spirit, families and friend groups are welcome to bring their own snacks and drinks and spend the day picnicking al fresco underneath the treetops during the summer months. You can even bring your canine companions along for the day – but they must first be vetted and approved by the arboretum administration.

Address 150 Rue Pine, Sainte-Anne-de-Bellevue, QC H9X 3L2, +1 (514) 398-7811, www.mcgill.ca/morganarboretum | **Getting there** By car, take the Autoroute 40 W to Voie de Service N in Sainte-Anne-de-Bellevue and continue onto Rue Saint-Marie to Rue Pine | **Hours** Daily 9am–4pm | **Tip** The Jardins des Floralies in Parc Jean-Drapeau (1 Circuit Gilles Villeneuve, www.parcjeandrapeau.com/en) was first established during the International Floralies competition of 1980 and offers a stunning display of local flora.

71 Musée des Ondes Emile Berliner

The history of electromagnetic waves

There's a good chance you'd walk right past the Musée des Ondes Emile Berliner without giving it much thought. The 1920s-era building at the northeast corner intersection of Rue Lenoir and Rue Saint Antoine looks like any other industrial building in the Saint Henri neighbourhood. But behind the frosted windows is one of the most important buildings of the technological revolution of the 20th century and in the history of recording and broadcasting.

The Musée des Ondes, or the Wave Museum *en anglais*, is housed in the former manufacturing site of Emile Berliner (1851–1929), known as the old RCA building, and pays tribute to the late inventor of the gramophone. The German American inventor founded the Berliner Gramophone Company of Canada in Montreal in 1899 and is regarded as one of the fathers of modern sound recording.

A dedicated group of senior volunteers, many of whom are retired historians and technicians, lend their time and expertise in order to classify, study, and even repair new artifacts coming into the museum. Each and every item has been hand-selected by people who are very familiar with the original product.

You'll find a mix of historically relevant and home-grown items and collections within the museum, all curated with the idea of providing visitors with a better understanding of the science of sound and electromagnetic waves. It's also an ode to the role that Montreal companies played in the cultural revolution of sound technology. You'll find hundred-year-old gramophones and artifacts from Berliner's personal collection, as well as rotating exhibits to freshen up the museum each year. The museum received the Governor General's History Award in 2020 for its contributions to the music industry, and it's easy to see why.

Address 1001 Rue Lenoir, Montreal, QC H4C 2Z6, +1 (514) 932-9663, www.moeb.ca/en, info@moeb.ca | Getting there Metro 2 to Place Saint-Henri (Orange Line); bus 17. 78. 371 to Saint-Antoine/Lenoir | Hours Mon–Fri 10am–4pm, Sat & Sun 2–5pm | Tip While in Saint-Henri, go see the large bronze and granite monument of Canadian strongman Louis Cyr in the Parc des Hommes-Forts (corner of Rue Saint-Antoine W and De Courcelle).

72 Mussolini Fresco
The only church to feature the dictator

The Church of the Madonna della Difesa in Montreal's Little Italy neighbourhood has a remarkable local and international history that goes beyond the Romanesque-style architecture and Roch Montbriant design. It's here that many members of the Montreal mafia families have been laid to rest. And the Italian-built church is also the only place of worship in the world that hosts a prominent fresco of fascist dictator Benito Mussolini.

Designed and painted by Italian Canadian artist Guido Nincheri before World War II, the fresco's representation of Benito Mussolini might seem questionable at first glance. But it was actually commissioned to commemorate his signing of the Lateran Treaty of 1929. The agreement, part of the Lateran Pacts between the Holy See and Italian King Victor Emmanuel III, with Mussolini as his prime minister, declared that the Vatican City State would become the pope's neutral and inviolable territory and guaranteed his political independence.

You may recognize the church from *Mambo Italiano* (2003) and other films. The century-old Church of the Madonna della Difesa was also named a National Historic Site of Canada in 2002 and continues to serve the oldest Italian community in the country. The large cupola and brick façade, combined with the easily recognizable (and slightly controversial) Guido Nincheri frescos, have positioned this church as one of the most infamous houses of prayer in North America.

The Roman Catholic church doesn't offer private tours or function as a museum in the way larger churches in Montreal sometimes do, but it does welcome visitors who are curious to get a better look at the architecture. Keep in mind that the Church of the Madonna della Difesa offers weekend and celebratory mass (in Italian), as well as weddings and funerals, and so it is not always open for guests to visit the interior.

Address 6800 Avenue Henri Julien, Montreal, QC H2S 2V4, www.diocesemontreal.org | Getting there Metro 2 to Beaubien (Orange Line); bus 55 to Saint-Laurent/Bélanger | Hours See website for hours and mass schedule | Tip Parc Dante (Rue Dante, https://montreal.ca/lieux/parc-dante) always has something going on – weekend flea markets, live music, dancers, open-air cinema, and various other festivities within the Italian community.

73__National Archives in Montreal

A stunning beaux arts bibliothèque

The National Archives in Montreal is one of the best spots to spend your time working remotely or unwinding with a good book. The stunning, early-1900s, beaux-arts-style building is just as captivating on the outside as it is on the inside, complete with grey limestone and pure-white, wrought-iron detailing.

The Old Port establishment is set in the former École des Hautes Études Commerciales (HEC) building, and today it serves as a national archive, housing key pieces of Quebecois history and documents dating back to the seventeenth century. The historic property is open to the public and periodically offers themed exhibits on different aspects of Quebec society both past and present, but it's the main atrium and study space that makes this address so magnificent. Just keep in mind that it's not a library, and its archives-related collections are only available for in-house reference use.

This archives centre is designed with its stacks laid out on the perimeter of multiple storeys, which gives an almost theatrical look to the light-flooded space. The open-concept main floor, complete with rows of mahogany desks and antique-inspired banker lamps, is available for the public to work or study in an elegant space brimming with Montreal history.

The architecturally rich environment makes for one of the most inspiring places for concentrating quietly in the city. But if you're not one for working in public, the National Archives in Montreal also provides free, French-language guided tours of the space on a regular basis (except in the summer). Reservations may be required. It also happens to be a pretty good site for snapping social media content. Just don't stage a full-fledged photo shoot – even if it's not a library, it's a space dedicated to quiet study.

Address 535 Avenue Viger E, Montreal, QC H2L 2P3, +1 800-363-9028 or +1 514 873-1100 (local number), www.banq.qc.ca | Getting there Metro 1, 2, 4 to Berri-UQAM (Green, Orange, Yellow Lines) or Metro 2 to Champ-de-Mars (Orange Line); bus 14, 150, 350, 355, 364, 445 to René-Lévesque/Saint-Hubert | Hours Mon & Tue, Thu & Fri 9am–5pm, Wed 9am–9pm | Tip The Islamic Studies Library (3485 Rue McTavish, www.mcgill.ca/library/branches/islamic) is the first of its kind in Quebec; an impressive collection of works on Islamic civilisation available in English, French, German, Dutch, Spanish, Italian, Russian, Arabic, Persian, Turkish (Ottoman and modern), Urdu, and Indonesian.

74 NHL Centre Ice
A piece of Habs history

It might not look like a gargantuan sports stadium these days, but the Montreal Forum was home to the Montreal Canadiens from 1926 to 1996 and the Montreal Maroons from 1924 to 1938. A total of 12 Stanley Cup championships were won on Forum ice. Despite its notoriety and relevance to the Montreal sporting community, these days it's mainly used as an entertainment venue, cinema, and shopping center.

Fortunately, the historic building still preserves a row of authentic Montreal Forum arena seating and a marker to note the precise location of the centre ice for fans in the know to visit and appreciate. Nods to the impressive history here is dotted through the entire building, with historic images and artifacts hidden in plain sight to help fans and history buffs transport themselves to the golden era of the NHL.

That said, this multiplex building looked a lot different back in the day than it does today. The Montreal Forum was named "the most storied building in hockey history" by *Sporting News* magazine, and although it might not seem grandiose today, it's important to remember that the sporting venue was built by the Canadian Arena Company in just 159 days – a flash in the pan in Montreal construction time. The 9,300-seat venue was later expanded to nearly 20,000 seats and became the default sporting venue for the National Hockey League, as well as various amateur leagues throughout the city.

The kicker? Throughout the decades-long history of this building, only two visiting teams won the Stanley Cup on Montreal Forum ice. The New York Rangers defeated the Montreal Maroons and nabbed the prize in 1928, while the Calgary Flames won the Cup in 1989, defeating the Montreal Canadiens. The last game here was played on March 11, 1996, when the Canadiens defeated the Dallas Stars 4-1 before the team moved down the street to what is now known as the Bell Centre.

Address 2313 Rue Saint-Catherine W, Montreal, QC H3H 1N2, +1 (514) 933-6786 | Getting there Metro 1 to Atwater (Green Line); bus 15, 356, 358 to Atwater | Hours Sun–Thu 6am–midnight, Fri & Sat 6–1am | Tip The Bell Centre (1909 Avenue des Canadiens-de-Montréal, www.centrebell.ca/en) is the current home of the Montreal Canadiens, and you'll find dozens of memorials, monuments, and plaques dedicated to the history of *Les Habitants*.

75   Notre Dame Basilica

Walk down the aisle where Celine Dion tied the knot

Musical superstar Celine Dion and René Angelil created a love story for the ages. The pair was married for 22 years before Angelil tragically died in 2016 following a battle with throat cancer. Dion met Angelil when she was just 12 years old and starting out in the industry. The pair became romantic when Dion was 19, eventually taking their love story public when she was 26. It was temporarily considered taboo, given that Angelil was Dion's manager, but the media would quickly move on once the marriage proved it would prevail.

The couple wed on December 17, 1994 at a private ceremony within the walls of the infamous Notre Dame Basilica in Old Montreal. The Roman Catholic Church has played home to a number of extravagant events, but Quebec's Queen of Pop garners the top spot for her romantic nuptials with her former manager and longtime partner. The bride wore a $25,000 hand-sewn dress made of French silk that took more than 1,000 hours to create. The dress had long sleeves fit for the cold Montreal air she would endure while entering and exiting the basilica to greet revved-up fans and romantics. The train measured 6 metres (20 feet).

Designed in Gothic Revival architecture style, the Notre Dame Basilica is internationally recognized as one of the most dramatic places of worship in the world, which is fitting for Dion. Although there isn't much public video of the pop singer's wedding to Angelil, it's easy to envision the romantic spectacle that went on behind closed doors. The Notre Dame Basilica dates back to 1829 and retains many of its original features, including a Casavant Frères pipe organ and a 10-bell carillon. The interior vaults feature deep blue hues with gold stars and, interestingly enough, stained glass windows that don't represent biblical events but rather major religious events throughout the city of Montreal.

Address 110 Rue Notre-Dame W, Montreal, QC H2Y 1T1, www.basiliquenotredame.ca/en | Getting there Metro 2 to 2 Place-d'Armes (Orange Line); bus 361 to Place Jacques-Cartier | Hours Mon–Fri 9am–4:30pm, Sat 9am–4pm, Sun 12:30–4pm | Tip Head further into Old Montreal to find the early 19th-century Notre-Dame-de-Bon-Secours (400 Rue Saint-Paul E, www.margueritebourgeoys.org), also known as the "Sailors' Church." It's the oldest church in the city and first functioned as a pilgrimage site for seafarers arriving at the Old Port.

76__Nouilles de Lan Zhou

Freshness is the name of the game

The tiny but mighty Nouilles de Lan Zhou is tucked onto the main floor of a grocery store at the south end of Chinatown. This noodle house is a must-visit for noodle fiends. The homemade soup destination hosts a spectacle in the front window so guests and passersby can stop and admire the art of hand-pulled noodles.

Owner Chris Yu-Ming Gao first opened Nouilles de Lan Zhou as a nod to his own family's Lanzhou noodle-making tradition. The art of the west-central Chinese noodle-making in particular has captured the hearts and stomachs of Chinatown regulars since the compact restaurant first opened its doors in 2014. In fact, Gao has since opened satellite restaurants across Canada, but it's the Saint Laurent location that has the most heart and soul - and also some of the most certified noodle masters!

Lanzhou noodle-making originated in Lanzhou, a city of about 1.5 million people in Mainland China. The traditional soup is usually eaten at breakfast, and it's served in thousands of shops across the Chinese city. Nouilles de Lan Zhou is better known as a lunch and dinner dining destination, but the restaurant retains the same noodle-pulling method and otherwise sticks with tradition. The wheat flour dough is pulled and swung in folds and loops until it transforms – seemingly by magic – into thin yet bouncy noodles. The noodles are then cooked for just 60 seconds, which allows them to remain chewy without becoming soggy in the accompanying broth.

The cozy dining room only has space for about 50 guests at a time with tables and chairs snaking their way around the open kitchen and alongside the escalator that leads into the downstairs G & D Supermarket. Due in part to the tiny dining space and also because of the fresh and umami-packed menu, you'll often run into a line that worms its way down Saint Laurent. But rest assured that it's always worth the wait.

Address 1006 Saint-Laurent Boulevard, Montreal, QC H2Z 9Y9, +1 (514) 800-2959, www.lanzhou.ca/montreal | Getting there Metro 2 to Place-d'Armes (Orange Line); bus 15, 80, 125, 480 to Place des Arts | Hours Mon–Thu 11am–9pm, Fri & Sat 11am–9:30pm | Tip Take the escalator downstairs to G & D Supermarket (1006 Boulevard Saint-Laurent, www.gdsupermarche.com), a well-appointed Asian grocery store that stocks everything from traditional Chinese medicine and Korean beauty products to colourful Japanese desserts and snacks.

77 Norman Bethune Square
A Canadian hero in China

You can't miss Norman Bethune Square. In fact, you'll probably see the hundreds of pigeons cooing and strutting their stuff before you recognize the towering monument at the corner of Guy and de Maisonneuve. The location of the square creates the perfect haven for pigeons ambling around the bustling Concordia University campus, but despite the distraction, Norman Bethune Square represents something a lot bigger. It's a symbol of public health in Canada and the amicable relations between China and Canada in the early 20th century.

The life-sized marble and granite monument in the centre of the square was a gift to the City of Montreal from the People's Republic of China in 1976 in thanks for Bethune's contribution and commitment to military health during Japan's invasion of China.

The Ontario-born Montrealer quickly became a revered doctor at McGill University's Royal Victoria Hospital, where he worked as a thoracic surgeon early on in his career. However, as he became more and more concerned with the socio-economic aspects of disease during the Great Depression, Bethune would seek out underprivileged Montrealers to give them free healthcare. He would frequently urge his colleagues at the hospital to do the same and was politically active in promoting the idea of socialized medicine in Canada.

In January 1938, frustrated by the state of affairs in Canadian medicine, Bethune travelled to China and joined the Chinese Communists led by Mao Zedong. He performed emergency surgical operations on both sides of the battlefield. Bethune was eventually stationed with the Communist Party of China's Eighth Route Army during the Japanese invasion, and, just short of two years after setting foot on Chinese soil, he tragically perished at the age of 49, from sepsis on the battlefield after cutting his finger while operating on a patient with a bacterial infection.

Address 2081 Rue Guy, Montreal, QC H3H 2L9 | **Getting there** Metro 1 to Guy-Concordia (Green Line); bus 24, 356 to Sherbrooke/Côte-des-Neiges | **Hours** Unrestricted | **Tip** The Musée des Fusiliers Mont-Royal (3721 Avenue Henri-Julien, www.lesfusiliersmont-royal.com) in the Plateau offers a curation of military history and artifacts from across the city, including uniforms, medals, and photography showing a slice of what life was like in peace and in war throughout the last century.

78 N Sur MacKay

Where everybody knows your name

Did you know that women weren't legally allowed in bars and public houses in Quebec until the late 1980s? Pubs and taverns were seen as the epitome of freedom for men, and letting their girlfriends and wives into such spaces was met with great resistance. Incredibly, it wasn't until 1986 that the actual law was amended to prohibit taverns from excluding female patrons.

Happily, this form of discrimination is a thing of the past, and it can be hard to even imagine such a time when you walk through the doors of N Sur Mackay. The female-owned and operated pub and specialty cocktail bar in the middle of downtown Montreal is a wonder to behold. Owner Natasha Geoffrion-Greenslade and her band of bartenders run a tight ship as a steady flow of regulars float into the sumptuous lounge for a delicate martini, a whiskey flight, or a hot boozy beverage, all served in ornate stemware and vintage, floral-hued teacups. The homey atmosphere feels like your cool aunt's home bar – if your cool aunt happened to be a mixologist with great taste in antique art and glassware, that is.

N Sur MacKay is one of those unique establishments in the downtown core that doesn't just cater to students passing by simply to get drunk, nor does it exclusively serve the downtown business set. Despite its position in the middle of the action, N is first and foremost a neighbourhood bar that, for the past decade, has been focused on creating a sense of comradery not just through cocktails but through conversations and community-building. You'll find all kinds of excuses to celebrate and get together with friends new and old here. There are expert-led whiskey tastings and Sip 'N Knit nights, where avid knitters can enjoy a glass or a pint while working on their latest project. You'll even see the occasional board game in the back room for those looking to bond over cards and dice.

Address 1244 Rue Mackay, Montreal, QC H3G 2H4, www.facebook.com/NsurMackay, info@nsurmackay.ca | Getting there Metro 1 to Guy-Concordia (Green Line) or Metro 2 to Lucien-L'Allier (Orange Line); bus 57, 166, 427, 165 to Guy/Sainte-Catherine | Hours Sun–Wed 4pm–1am, Thu–Sat 1pm–3am | Tip Head down the street to visit the Ring (Corner of Avenue McGill College and Rue Cathcart, www.placevillemarie.com/en/the-ring), a controversial art installation by Quebec architect Claude Cormier. The towering piece of art changed the face of Esplanade Place Ville Marie.

79___Old Port Fishing

Get hooked on downtown fishing

Pass by any lake during the winter months in Quebec, and you'll notice colourful, little huts out on the frozen sheaths of ice. The province of Quebec is famous for ice fishing, or *pêche blanche*, a practice rooted in Indigenous culture that has grown into a common pastime for anyone looking for a meditative way to get out and enjoy the crisp winter months. Pêche Vieux-Montréal, or Fishing Old Montreal, once offered ice fishing to tourists and locals interested in getting to know the culture, but with the changing climate, the waters have not frozen over sufficiently in recent years.

That doesn't mean you have to forego the art of Quebecois fishing though. Guests can still experience the relaxing atmosphere in the middle of the city, and the folks at Pêche aim to make the experience as simple as possible, even if you've never fished before. From May through December, their highly trained anglers with over 20 years of experience in professional fishing tournaments will show you how it's done during half- or full-day excursions for up to four people. You're guaranteed to catch a fish, or your guided experience is free (provided the conditions are normal).

Your guide will take you out to the best spot to catch dinner, and you'll be right in the middle of the Old Port rather than on a countryside lake. Despite the sights and sounds of the city, the fishing experience will be surprisingly relaxing. Your guide will walk you through each step of the way, and the full-day experience should give you a good idea of what to expect while fishing if you decide to take the hobby up on your own.

Although Quebec is internationally recognized for its tommy cod fishing in Saint-Anne-de-la-Pérade, you're more likely to catch walleye, bass, carp, or northern pike in the city centre. Whichever fish you catch, it will taste especially delicious because you reeled it in yourself.

Address 101 Chemin de la Rive, Longueuil, QC J4H 4C9, +1 (514) 715-7773, www.fishingom.com, pechevm2019@gmail.com | **Getting there** Bus 17, 25, 76 to Du Bord-de-l'Eau Ouest/Grant | **Hours** See website for reservations | **Tip** The pick-up spot for Peche Vieux-Montreal is right next to Rue Saint-Charles W in the heart of Vieux Longueuil (www.longueuil.quebec). Take a walk down the charming neighbourhood street and marvel at the architecture and distant views of the Montreal skyline.

80 Oscar Peterson Mural

An homage to the late king of Canadian jazz

Most people are quick to set their sights on New Orleans or New York when conjuring up images of the birthplace of jazz. But they're doing themselves a disservice to overlook the impact that Montreal has had on the greater jazz industry. Oscar Peterson, largely considered one of the best jazz musicians of all time, was born and raised in working-class Montreal in 1925 and set the stage for the jazz scene in the early aughts of Montreal's Sin City era in the 1940s and 50s.

"I had to teach myself by being around the jazz that was being played in Montreal at that time. And there were quite a few good players," Peterson famously said of the influence that his hometown had on his craft and musical prowess. Although Peterson eventually moved south of the border to further his career as a musician and performer, Montreal still held a close place in his heart as the city where he first planted his roots for what would become a long and well-respected musician journey.

Oscar Peterson's legacy lives on in the Montreal jazz community, and the *Jazz Born Here* mural outside of his childhood stomping ground comes as a visual reminder of the impact the jazz legend made on the Little Burgundy neighbourhood and beyond. The monument located on the corner of Saint Jacques and des Seigneurs was created in 2011 by Montreal artist Gene Pendon to commemorate the fifth anniversary of Peterson's passing but it also serves as a point of pride for the current community and its deeply rooted musical heritage.

Pendon pulled images directly from Peterson's personal family archives in order to breathe life into the visual homage, while also using motifs from various points in Peterson's career and more general jazz references. Your eye will follow the blue, black, and purple colorways to the ascending piano that is meant to represent Peterson's own rise to stardom and his lasting legacy.

Address 1855 Rue Saint-Jacques, Montreal, QC H3J 1Y2, www.artpublicmontreal.ca |
Getting there Metro 2 to Georges-Vanier (Orange Line); bus 36, 57 to Guy/Saint-Jacques |
Hours Unrestricted | Tip Grab a drink and take in the views at the Château Champlain
Hotel (1050 Rue De La Gauchetière W, www.marriott.com), the exact crossroads where
Peterson got his big break at the now-defunct Alberta Lounge.

81__Pang Pang Karaoke

A night of karaoke – without the stage fright

When you think of karaoke night, what comes to mind? For most of us, it involves some sort of sticky dive bar, a stage in the middle of the room, and an abundance of liquid courage. Let's just say that Western-style karaoke isn't for the faint of heart, and so many folks overlook the surprisingly fun activity simply due to stage fright.

That's where Pang Pang Karaoke comes in. Instead of a main stage and a huge audience, the Korean-owned and operated karaoke venue takes inspiration from South Korean and Japanese-style karaoke and instead rents out small and medium-sized private rooms for groups looking to belt it out in the company of close friends only.

The venue off a quiet stretch of Rue Mackay feels like a psyche-delic hotel lobby, complete with a brass fountain and enough flashing lights and neon LEDs to beckon singers and wannabe musicians to come in from outer space. Once you set foot within the four walls of the intimate singing rooms, the magic really starts to happen.

Manager and owner Kimi Lee aims to create an atmosphere that feels safe and fun for friends and colleagues to let loose without the stress and anxiety that can sometimes come with putting on a public performance for an entire bar. The winding hallway features num-bered rooms, much like a hotel, that range from small spaces suit-able for close friends all the way up to VIP suites that can fit up to 20 guests at a time.

Every neon-hued singing room is decked out with a variety of disco lights, flashing LEDs, and a leatherbound songbook that includes everything from country ballads and 90s hits to current radio songs and, of course, plenty of K-pop. Enter a song via the oversized remote control, and it pops up onto the large TV screen, with its own cheeky Korean music video in the background that keeps guests entertained and singing along until it's their turn at the mic.

Address 1226 Rue Mackay, Montreal, QC H3G 2H4, +1 (514) 938-8886, www.pangpangkaraoke.com | **Getting there** Metro 1 to Guy-Concordia (Green Line) or Metro 2 to Lucien-L'allier (Orange Line) | **Hours** Mon–Thu & Sun 3pm–1am, Fri & Sat 3pm–3am | **Tip** Pang Pang Karaoke doesn't offer alcoholic beverages, so if you want a little liquid courage before singing, head three doors down to Upstairs Jazz Bar & Grill (1254 Rue Mackay, www.upstairsjazz.com) for a cocktail while taking in the smooth sounds of local jazz musicians.

82 Parc Ahuntsic

Universally accessible fun for all

You might assume that all children's playgrounds are designed to support and uplift all children. But a well-designed and inclusive playground requires extra forethought and care. Inclusive and sensory-rich parks and playgrounds allow children of all abilities to be kids. These spaces also help foster a greater sense of community and have the ability to become multi-generational destinations where everyone, regardless of age or health, can enjoy, participate, and play.

The University of Buffalo School of Architecture and Planning describes this kind of inclusive and universal design as a "process that enables and empowers a diverse population by improving human performance, health and wellness, and social participation." The universally accessible play gym at Parc Ahuntsic checks off all those boxes and then some, thanks to its assistive devices, like swings with special parent-child seats, just-right challenges, gently sloping and low-to-the-ground slides, and easily accessible washrooms onsite.

Parc Ahuntsic is situated in the Ahuntsic-Cartierville borough right next to the Terminus Henri-Bourassa. The 10-hectare (25-acre) community space is designed to be fully immersive for families and really anyone in search of green space in the North Island. There are also dedicated paths for both pedestrians and cyclists, a skate park, an indoor skating rink, sledding in the winter, and a bowling green with various lawn games. The park has become a neighbourhood favourite on hot summer days, thanks to its child-friendly wading pool, splash pads, and fountains.

There's a lot to explore within the boundaries of the sprawling public park, and even though there's much to do and see, you should look for the natural splendour built into the community space. Be sure to give yourself time to enjoy the greenery, and maybe even pack a picnic to enjoy by the pond.

Address 10555 Rue Lajeunesse, Montreal, QC H3L 2E4, +1 (514) 872-0311, https://montreal.ca/en/places/parc-ahuntsic | Getting there Metro 2 to Henri-Bourassa (Orange Line); bus 35, 361 to Lajeunesse/Prieur | Hours Daily 6am – midnight | Tip The Van Horne Skatepark (5855 Boulevard Saint-Laurent) is the first multi-purpose, youth-oriented facility of its kind in the Plateau and features benches, removable modules, and effect lighting for special events.

83 Parc Jeanne Mance

A park for all with land-locked beach volleyball

Le Plateau-Mont-Royal is perhaps one of the best neighbourhoods in the city to spend a lazy summer day. The terrasse-dotted pedestrian streets, boutiques, and open-air cafés make this walkable part of town a desirable destination for *bon vivants* from all over the city. When the dog days of summer begin to blanket Montreal in a sun-fueled haze, it's Parc Jeanne Mance that offers the most reprieve (especially with a picnic and a couple of dep beers in hand).

The history of Parc Jeanne Mance dates all the way back to the end of the 19th century, when it was known as Fletcher's Field, a cow pasture owned by a farmer named Fletcher. The park was also used as a military parade ground and a practice area for the Montreal Lacrosse Club and Royal Montreal Golf Club. Eventually it was renamed in recognition of the founder of the neighbouring Hôtel-Dieu de Montréal and became a public green space for Montrealers to enjoy.

The centrally located park, which officially runs along Avenue Parc between Pine and Mount Royal, serves as an easily accessible meeting point that ties the Plateau neighbourhood with downtown Montreal and the mouth of Mount Royal. It comes as no surprise that this park is where major demonstrations, drumming and dancing with the Tam Tams, and many an after-work, alfresco *cinq à sept* tend to take place.

However, although the park is well-known as a watering hole and gathering spot for friends and families to spread out a picnic blanket and bask in the sun, it's also home to plenty of sports-focused offerings, including four well-maintained beach volleyball courts right in the middle of the city. Parc Jeanne Mance hosts a series of casual beach volleyball tournaments throughout the summer. It's also open for those looking to try their hand at the sport on a casual basis. Who said you had to live by the sea in order to partake in beach sports?

Address 4422 Avenue Esplanade, Montreal, QC H2W 2N4, https://montreal.ca/lieux/
parc-jeanne-mance | Getting there Metro 2 to Mont-Royal (Orange Line); bus 80, 129,
365 480 to Monument à sir George-Étienne-Cartier | Hours Daily 6am–midnight |
Tip The Jean-Doré Beach in Parc Jean-Drapeau (1 Circuit Gilles Villeneuve,
www.parcjeandrapeau.com/en) is the seasonal home to Aquazilla, a massive, 30-by-35-meter
(100-by-115 foot), inflatable structure on the water, with a giant swing, monkey bars, and
central trampoline in the middle of the man-made beach.

84 The Peace Treaty of 1701
The alleged end to a century of hostility

There are quite a few major historical events that are conveniently absent from our history books and our collective memory. The signing of the Peace Treaty at Place de la Grande-Paix-de-Montréal is one of those significant moments that seemingly missed the history book deadline. It was only in the late '90s that research and social initiatives revived this pivotal agreement between New France and 1,300 representatives from 39 of the First Nations of North America.

Let's look a few centuries back in time. It's the turn of the 18th century, and war and hostility has been brewing between New France and the region's First Nations for nearly a hundred years. The conflict was first initiated in 1609 by Samuel de Champlain, who essentially pushed the French into a pre-existing world of alliances and enemies within Indigenous communities as a ploy to strengthen New France's stakes in the fur trade.

When Louis-Hector de Callière was promoted from the governor of Montreal – and later the governor of all New France – he immediately went to work to end the decades-long war. Two years later, the Peace Treaty of 1701 was signed and provided peace across the region for decades until the British conquest of New France in 1760.

Many years later in 1999, when research and other initiatives uncovered the historical importance of this document, the city commemorated the 300th anniversary of the event by renaming a portion of Place d'Youville to Place de la Grande-Paix-de-Montréal. It's marked by an obelisk that both honours the founders of the city and also indicates the exact location where the treaty was signed. The peace treaty itself is locked away at the nearby Montreal Museum of Archaeology and History, but the permanent plaques dotted throughout the public square in the Old Port synthesize the momentous event for passersby to appreciate.

Address Place d'Youville, Montreal, QC H2Y 2N9 | Getting there Metro 2 to Place-d'Armes (Orange Line); bus 35, 61, 168 to Square-Victoria-OACI | Hours Daily 8am–11pm | Tip The Maison Nivard-De Saint-Dizier (7244 Boulevard LaSalle, www.maisonnivard-de-saint-dizier.com) in Verdun offers a glimpse at what 18th-century New France architecture looked like – but it's also the largest prehistoric archeological site on the island of Montreal with artifacts that date back more than 5,000 years.

85 Penguins in the Plateau
Peep the penguins in the window

The Plateau-Mont-Royal has a reputation for being one of the most architecturally beautiful and liveliest boroughs in the city. Its quaint and colourful houses, vintage shops, and abundance of restaurants and entertainment venues make it a desirable destination to live or visit. But it's the people who live here and their whimsical antics that are the beating heart of the neighbourhood. Case in point: Dominique Juge and her collection of penguins.

Wandering down the quiet Rue de Mentana between Napoleon and Duluth Est, most people are struck by the unique architecture and mature trees that dot the quintessentially Rue Plateau. But don't miss the miniature waddle of penguins that began by fluke back in the 1990s, when Juge received a big wooden penguin statue from her daughter. That gift bird started her on a mission to collect and display as many penguins as possible. You can currently see over a hundred penguins of all shapes, sizes, and species in her bite-sized window looking out onto the street.

"I started collecting penguins because I think it's a beautiful animal, and the children love it," Dominique explains. "I'm always afraid they'll break the window because some are very enthusiastic!" The collection has been on display for the past 30 years, and although Juge has had to stop actively collecting the subantarctic birds, she regularly receives gifts in the form of penguins from people in the neighbourhood who have come to love the collection too. In fact, one family gives her a new penguin every Halloween in thanks for brightening their corner of the world.

Take the time to appreciate this micro-sized neighbourhood institution packed with penguins and marvel at just how many of the little birds have been added to the space. Can you spot the gentoos? The chinstraps? What about the emperor penguins? It's a veritable expedition to Antarctica!

Address 3918 Rue de Mentana, Montreal, QC H2L 3R8 | Getting there Metro 2 to
Sherbrooke (Orange Line); bus 14 to Du Park-La-Fontaine/Napoleon | Hours Unrestricted
from the outside | Tip Visit the largest colony of rockhopper penguins in North America
at the Biodôme (4777 Avenue Pierre-de Coubertin, www.espacepourlavie.ca/en/biodome),
which replicates the subantarctic habitat in order to preserve the endangered penguin species.

86 Place Marie-Josèphe Angélique

The immortal face of liberation

In order to understand the significance of Place Marie-Josèphe Angélique, you'll need to travel 300 years into the past and accept some ugly truths about Canada's history of enslavement. Marie-Josèphe Angélique (ca. 1705 – 1734), a Portuguese-born Black woman, was taken to New France, where French businessman François Poulin de Francheville and his wife Thérèse de Couagne enslaved her. She refused to believe that she couldn't realize her dreams of returning to her birthplace, and she would ultimately lose her life in the pursuit of freedom.

Held in slavery for most of her days, Angélique was nonetheless outspoken and passionate. She and her lover, a white indentured servant named Claude Thibault, attempted to escape from Montreal multiple times, hiding in Longueuil or Châteauguay before being caught and brought back to the Francheville household.

There's no way to know for sure exactly what happened next. But around seven o'clock in the evening on Saturday, April 10, 1734, a fire broke out at the Francheville estate and subsequently burnt down 45 houses in the immediate area. Angélique was found guilty of setting the fire as a distraction to help facilitate her escape. She was tortured and publicly executed. But she never revealed the name of her lover to the judge or the notary.

Angélique's life and legacy have given way to a wealth of creative tributes and odes to the Canadian hero, including multiple novels, history books, plays, songs, and even films. In 2012, the public square between the Champ-de-Mars metro station and the Montreal City Hall was named Place Marie-Josèphe-Angélique in her honour. Yet these many years later, there's still no official signage or plaques to commemorate the rebel and exceptionally strong-minded woman.

Address Avenue Viger E, Montreal, QC H2Y 3Z8 | Getting there Metro 2 to Champ-de-Mars (Orange Line); bus 360 to Viger/De l'Hôtel-de-Ville | Hours Unrestricted | Tip The Afromusée (533 Rue Ontario E, www.afromusee.org) is the leading institution for African and Afro-descendant culture in Montreal, where you'll find a curation of artwork, records of memory, and artifacts designed to promote and raise the visibility of these communities in Canada.

87 Princess Theatre

Houdini was sucker-punched here

Jocelyn Gordon Whitehead certainly isn't a household name. He's not a famous Montrealer or a particularly noteworthy addition to our history books. You've probably never even heard of him. But friends and fans of Harry Houdini will never forget this problematic Montrealer. Whitehead was born and bred in Montreal and a seemingly average university student at McGill. But that all changed on October 22, 1926, the night one unknown man allegedly sucker-punched one world-famous magician and performer.

For Houdini, the routine, death-defying magic show at the Princess Theatre on Sainte-Catherine was just another night of show business before he would be heading to the US to continue his headline tour. But Whitehead had other plans. While Houdini was performing in Montreal, he had been invited to give a talk down the street at McGill University about his recent work in debunking a Boston medium. Whitehead and Samuel J. Smilovitz, another student, reportedly visited Houdini in his dressing room after the lecture. They'd decided they wanted to beat Houdini at his own game.

During the brief encounter, Whitehead allegedly wanted to test Houdini's incredible strength and asked him if it was true that he could absorb punches without harm. It's believed that Houdini humoured the student and allowed Whitehead to hit him with his best shot. However, before Houdini was able to prepare himself, Whitehead struck the magician with three punches straight to the stomach. The magician died nine days later, on Halloween no less, due to an undetected case of appendicitis that was allegedly aggravated by the sucker punch in Montreal.

The former Princess Theatre renamed Le Parisien in 1963 now sits empty. Despite its position in the heart of the downtown core, the location has never been able to retain businesses. Paranormal experts believe it's haunted by Houdini's ghost.

Address 480 Rue Sainte-Catherine W, Montreal, QC H3B 1A6 | Getting there
Metro 1 to McGill (Green Line) | Hours Unrestricted from the outside only | Tip Pop
directly across the street to Marché Aux Fleurs MTL (459 Rue Sainte-Catherine W,
www.marcheauxfleursmtl.com/en), where you'll find a gorgeous selection of small plants
and floral arrangements tucked into a charming greenhouse-inspired glass kiosk.

88 Prison des Patriotes

Centuries of crime and punishment

You might not expect to find a century-old prison tucked into one of the most scenic areas of the city, but the site of the former Prison des Patriotes au Pied-du-Courant at the Musée National des Patriotes is located right along the banks of the Saint Lawrence River, below the Jacques Cartier Bridge. To look at it, you'd think it was more of a historic building of architectural merit than one of the city's most notoriously grisly destinations when it came to crime and punishment.

The prison was built in 1835 by English-born architect John Wells (1789–1864), who was inspired by the Eastern State Penitentiary in Philadelphia, Pennsylvania. The neoclassical structure was developed to house 276 prisoners, but more than a thousand people would be incarcerated here during and after the Lower Canada Rebellion (1837–1838) against British rule. Today, the facility is owned by the Société des alcools du Québec (SAQ) and is host to both the prison museum and the liquor board's offices.

As you walk through the front doors of the museum, you might notice an ominous and hair-raising sensation – and you're definitely not imagining it. The history of the Prison des Patriotes is laid out for visitors to get a visual sense of the spine-tingling atmosphere through the carefully curated signage and the recreations of the prison itself, including what the average prison cell looked like, all backlit within the actual halls where prisoners were once held.

After you've done your time in Pied-du-Courant, make sure to visit the outdoor monument dedicated to the 12 members of the *Parti patriote* who were hanged for high treason. Created by prolific Quebecois artist and sculptor Alfred Laliberté (1877–1953), the pyramidal monument was designed to evoke an allegorical depiction of *Liberty with Broken Wings*. It now rests on the approximate coordinates where the patriots were killed.

Address 903 Avenue De Lorimier, Montreal, QC H2K 3V9, +1 (450) 787-3623, www.mndp.qc.ca, info@mndp.qc.ca | Getting there Metro 1 to Papineau (Green Line); bus 150 to De Lorimier/René-Lévesque | Hours See website for seasonal hours | Tip Bring your bike and hop on La Route Verte (2049 Rue Notre-Dame E, www.routeverte.com/en), which conveniently circles around the former prison grounds, opening up to the South Shore, the West Island, Laval, past Montreal, and into greater Quebec.

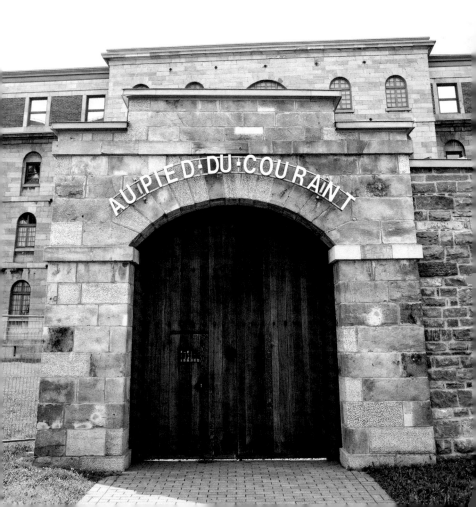

89__Provigo Fortin Crane
A nod to our railway history

Montreal has its fair share of historic farmers' markets and cheese shops dotted all over dozens of neighbourhoods. This is a city of passionate gourmands after all! But the historical relevance of the Provigo Fortin in Rosemont highlights a different part of Montreal's history. You'll notice almost immediately that this big-box grocery store looks and feels a little different from the average super-sized market.

The distinct change in architecture and urban planning is palpable at the CPR Angus Shops, and that's not necessarily an accident. The neighbourhood shopping complex dates back to the early 20th century when it functioned as a railcar manufacturing and repairing shop for the Canadian Pacific Railway (CPR). The repair site was built by Scottish Canadian financier and vice president of the CPR Richard B. Angus (1831–1922), and would see trains travelling into the East End of Montreal for repair and inspection before leaving the island.

However, the Angus Shops were decommissioned 1992, and the sprawling plot was redeveloped to suit commercial usage and still functions as a quasi-shopping complex today. The Provigo Fortin is the best example of the site's former railroad days. This is where you'll find the red brick-lined skeleton and steel buttress structure of the original CPR Angus Locoshop building visible from aisle to aisle.

But the star of the show is truly the full-sized railroad crane arm that seemingly dangles between the produce and natural foods aisle. The high-capacity overhead cranes were mainly used at the Angus Shops to lift heavy engines and steel wheels. Look up to see these words painted in French overhead, "Take care of yourself. Don't take any chances." They were meant to remind workers to stay aware of their environment. Today, they offer something to think about as you push your shopping cart along the aisles.

Address 2925 Rue Rachel E, Montreal, QC H1W 3Z8, +1 (514) 522-4442, www.provigo.ca/store-locator | Getting there Metro 1 to Préfontaine (Green Line); bus 25, 97 to Rachel/Dézéry | Hours Daily 8am–10pm | Tip Miami Deli down the street (3090 Rue Sherbrooke E, www.miamideli.com) is a whimsical Florida-themed restaurant that is just the right amount of kitsch with replica iguanas, palm trees, and swordfish hanging from all nooks and crannies.

90 The Pullman Chandelier

Eye-catching effervescence

Tucked behind an unassuming set of doors on the corner of Parc and Sherbrooke, Pullman is one of Montreal's very first wine bars. Owners Bruno Braën and Catherine Bélanger, of Pinard et Filles Vineyard, saw a lack of decent wines in the city when they opened their venue in 2004, and they have been serving a mix of natural wine and their personal favorites ever since. In this city of wine drinkers, Montrealers responded. The trailblazing wine bar sits anywhere from 60 to 250 clients a night throughout the unique upstairs/downstairs mezzanines and within the cozy nooks and crannies.

You'll first notice that Pullman's interior design is as singular in concept as the wine bar itself, along with the fun and sophisticated atmosphere that has been expertly achieved within a relatively small space. The entire dining room was designed by Braën with the intention of creating something that would be both timeless and unlike anything else in the city. He didn't want the space to look like other trendy wine bars from the early 2000s, and so he came up with his own signature design and décor. His aesthetic sense is expressed in the leather-backed chairs, dramatic drapery, and solid wood bar tops that create a look and atmosphere unique to Pullman.

The centrepiece of the entire dining space is without a doubt the sparkling, wine-glass chandelier that hangs high above the entrance of the restaurant. The chandelier was also the brainchild of Braën, who wanted to fill this space with something spectacular that would catch your eye as soon as you walked in – and something that would also be relevant to the establishment.

Nothing says "wine bar" more than a singularly wonderful chandelier made entirely of wine glasses. There are close to 200 glasses on this grand chandelier, a mix of Champagne flutes, grappa glasses, and port glasses, all dangling just overhead, keeping an eye on thirsty clientele below, and lighting up the environment.

Address 3424 Avenue du Parc, Montreal, QC H2X 2H5, +1 (514)-288-7779, www.pullman-mtl.com, info@pullman-mtl.com | Getting there Metro 1 to Place-des-Arts (Green Line); bus 80, 129, 365, 480 to Sherbrooke/De Bleury | Hours Wed & Thu 4:30–10pm, Fri & Sat 4:30–11pm | Tip At the corner of Avenue Président-Kennedy and Rue Jeanne-Mance, you'll find the oldest still-visible mural in Montreal, (2022 Rue Jeanne-Mance, www.artpublicmontreal.ca), an untitled work painted by Claude Dagenais and Jacques Sabourin in 1972.

91　René Lévesque Park
A spectacular open-air oeuvre

The importance of appreciating artwork isn't talked about enough these days. But whether you consider yourself an art aficionado or you can't tell your Édouard Manets from your Claude Monets, just being subjected to different forms of artwork opens up the stream of consciousness, stimulates conversation, and helps us to better understand culture and society, both past and present. Art and history go hand in hand, after all.

The city of Montreal is home to more than 40 different museums and countless galleries, which makes it easy for people of all ages to soak in the history and benefits of fine art. However, the city is also host to plenty of open-air cultural centres that are free of charge and just as filled with history and beauty as the indoor galleries and museums.

One such venue is the René Lévesque Park. The stunning peninsula offers panoramic views of the St. Lawrence River and Lake Saint-Louis, where the waterways crash against the shoreline. It also provides a pretty decent stand-in for the ocean, given Montreal's position hundreds of kilometres from the Atlantic Coast. The sprawling outdoor space is popular for family barbecues in the summertime and cross-country skiing come winter. However, the outdoor sculpture garden there should be on everyone's list of weekend strolls.

The Musée plein air de Lachine at the tip of the peninsula is one of the largest outdoor sculpture museums in Canada, with more than 22 different works of art set along the picturesque banks of the river. After acquiring artworks from various international and Quebecois artists in the mid-80s, including Graham Cantieni and Gilles Boisvert, the 14-hectare (35-acre) green space hosted the Salon international de la sculpture extérieure de Montréal in 1992 and again in 1994 and has since become the premiere open-air home for large-form sculptures in Quebec.

Address 398 Chemin du Canal, Lachine, QC H8S 4G2, +1 (514) 872-0311, https://montreal.ca/en/places/parc-rene-levesque | Getting there By car, take the Autoroute 20 West to exit 1re Avenue/Av. Dollard and follow Rue Saint-Patrick to destination | Hours Daily 6am–11pm | Tip The Lachine Canal network of bike paths (parks.canada.ca/lhn-nhs/qc/canallachine/activ/sentiers-trails) stretches 15 kilometres (9 miles) of paved, flat and fully off-road trails from downtown to Lachine. Hop on the bike path in the Old Port and weave your way to René Lévesque Park while taking in beautiful views of the water along the way.

92 The Roundhouse Café

Bannock, maple lattes, and more Indigenous treats

Blink and you might miss the quaint Roundhouse Café, or Café Maison ronde, tucked in the outskirts of Cabot Square Park. The small, takeout-style counter took over an old *vespasienne* (yes, urinal) just next to Atwater Metro and turned it into a snack bar and coffee shop. The only Indigenous café in the city, Roundhouse aims to celebrate First Nations and Inuit culinary specialties while promoting and empowering Indigenous culture through food and drink.

Whether you're looking to relax in the sun and enjoy a refreshing iced coffee in the park, or you're in the mood for food, Roundhouse has something to suit your fancy. The café specializes in modern Indigenous cuisine, including both salty and sweet Bannock, Totem Pole sandwiches, Mohawk-style salad, and a savoury treat known as an "Indian Taco," which you can sometimes find with venison or bison meat rather than more typical beef.

The indoor/outdoor coffee shop and takeout counter comes equipped with a handful of colourful tables and chairs set up on the edge of Cabot Square Park, which makes it an attractive option if you're hoping to enjoy casual outdoor dining downtown. Due to its small stature and outdoor-exclusive dining options, the Roundhouse Café is open exclusively from May to October, but the miniature restaurant hopes that its accessible approach to Indigenous cuisine will help break down barriers and make First Nations and Inuit culture and culinary offerings a much more talked-about experience within the Greater Montreal community.

The downtown square surrounding the Roundhouse Café is home to a large percentage of the Indigenous homeless population in the city, and, with the help of magazine *L'Itinéraire*, which employs quite a number of people experiencing homelessness, the proceeds from the café go toward helping this population and other underprivileged individuals in the city.

Address 2330 Rue Sainte-Catherine O, Montreal, QC H3H 1N2, +1 (514) 872-9465, www.itineraire.ca/roundhouse-cafe | Getting there Metro 1 to Atwater (Green Line) | Hours May–Oct Mon & Tue, Thu & Fri 9am–4pm | Tip Immerse yourself in more Indigenous culture by paying a visit to La Guilde (1356 Rue Sherbrooke W, www.laguilde.com/en), the non-profit Golden Square Mile art gallery with one of the most expansive collections of Inuit and First Nations artwork in the city.

93 Royal Montreal Curling

More than two centuries of sweeping

The Royal Montreal Curling Club first opened its doors over 200 years ago, during the reign of Britain's King George III, when Montreal was home to a mere 12,000 residents. This is the oldest curling club in North America and also the oldest active athletic club of any kind on the continent.

In his book, *The First Two Hundred Years: A History of the Royal Montreal Curling Club, 1807-2007*, author Donald G. Wallace writes that "twenty Scottish merchants and a chaplain who liked to curl together" sat down in Gillis Tavern and came up with the idea of establishing a curling club. And so the Montreal Curling Club was conceived on January 22, 1807 out of the need for a year-round reprieve where these curling fans could spend their time practicing the sport in an area protected from the weather, rather than on the open ice on the St. Lawrence River, where they normally met. "Royal" was added to the name on February 23, 1924, when a Royal Warrant granted the club the right, according to Wallace.

The members-only facility hosts regular leagues and competitions throughout the year for beginner and intermediate curlers to professional-level athletes. The club has played home to plenty of professional tournaments, having hosted and presented hundreds of cups throughout its lengthy history.

The club also sees itself as a space for welcoming new and curious curlers who might not have had the chance to try the sport otherwise. You can sign up for seasonal lessons if you want to try the sport, or take a drop-in lesson just to get a feel for the ice before committing to regular classes. Every second Friday evening, the club is open to anyone who wants to try curling individually. All you need is an open mind, a dry pair of shoes, and a comfortable pair of workout pants, and you're good to hit the ice. Everything else, from gear to expertise, will be provided for you.

Address 1850 Boulevard de Maisonneuve W, Montreal, QC H3H 1J8, +1 (514) 935-3411, www.royalmontrealcurling.ca | Getting there Metro 1 to Guy (Green Line); bus 57 to Guy-Concordia | Hours Mon–Fri 9am–6pm, Sat & Sun 9am–10pm | Tip Catch local bagpiper Jenna Dennison doing her thing at Holt Renfrew Ogilvy (1307 Rue Saint-Catherine W, www.holtrenfrew.com/en/store-events), the luxury department store that preserves its Scottish heritage with regular, complimentary bagpiping performances.

94 The Saint-Léonard Cavern
The star of the speleological society

You don't have to travel to Kentucky or New Mexico in the United States in order to explore the wonders of an underground cave network. In fact, you don't even need to leave the island of Montreal to find incredible cavernous experiences. Quietly nestled underneath Pie-XII Park in the Saint-Léonard borough, the Saint-Léonard Cavern was discovered over 200 years ago by a local farmer.

The hidden underground cave is thought to be over 15,000 years old. It has served as a hidden armoury and weapons cache during the Patriote Rebellion of 1837, but it was eventually sealed off and deemed unsafe 1968 to 1978 due to too many thrill seekers trespassing illegally. After this decade of solitude though, members of Quebec's Speleological Society won their fight to have the Saint-Léonard Cavern reopened for research purposes. After being designated as a "heritage site of regional interest" by the Montreal Urban Community in 1988, the site opened for guided public tours as well.

The cave was considered by most standards to be quite small for much of its history, measuring just 35 metres (115 feet) long and 8 metres (26 feet) deep. But then a second portion of the cave was discovered in 2017, which extended more than 250 metres (820 feet) in length. Local speleologists expect the total length of the cave will expand even further through ongoing exploration and research. This means that the area of the cave you visit today might not be the same one you'll see in the future.

Reservations are mandatory in order for members of the general public to enter the depths of the cavern, which is only open for the warmer months of the year. Your comprehensive guided tour will be led by a certified and experienced speleologist. You'll want to be sure to wear layers, even in the summertime, as the temperature in the cave stays at about 5 degrees Celsius year-round.

Address 5200 Boulevard Lavoisier, Saint-Léonard, QC H1R 1J2, +1 (514) 252-3006, www.speleo.qc.ca/reserver | Getting there Bus 136, 188 to Viau/Lavoisier | Hours See website for seasonal hours | Tip Explore surrounding Pie-XII Park (5200 Boulevard Lavoisier) as well. The family-friendly park features an outdoor skating rink in the winter and an outdoor swimming pool and tennis courts come summertime.

95_ The Secret Towers House
This Old House

This short, one-way street running between de Maisonneuve and Sainte Catherine in the centre of downtown hosts a handful of squat apartment buildings and nothing else particularly noteworthy. However, take a closer look, and you'll notice an old but perfectly preserved, two-storey, Victorian home nestled among the looming residential complexes. This house holds a secret.

The formerly abandoned stone home underwent a meticulous restoration complete with near-identical replicas of the outdoor woodwork and stained glass window detailing. But you won't find anyone at home here, as the house now hosts the Rue Towers mechanical ventilation station (MVS) for the nearby Société de transport de Montréal (STM) metro system.

This MVS is part of the STM's larger program to refurbish metro facilities and equipment. The building was acquired by the STM in 2017, and the four-year renovation project preserved its heritage and also solved the issue of finding substantial space and land for such a project in the middle of the downtown core. You can't tell from the outside, but the MVS is six times larger underground than it appears at street level. Below the two-storey home, four additional levels were built underground and required the excavation of more than 10,000 cubic metres (13,080 cubic yards) of soil and rock.

Although the heritage home sat empty for years before the STM began working on the MVS project, it was important to the architects and engineers to preserve the integrity of the original architecture, even if the interior of the home has been completely changed. Each individual stone was removed and numbered before being reinstalled on the front of the building. As you walk past this secret ventilation station, you'll also notice some lighting in the front hall, which further helps to create the illusion that someone might actually be living inside.

Address 1423 Rue Towers, Montreal, QC H3H 2E2 | Getting there Metro 1 to Guy-Concordia (Green Line) | Hours Unrestricted from the outside | Tip Exporail (110 Rue Saint-Pierre, www.exporail.org) is the biggest railway museum in Canada, offering visitors a permanent collection packed with railway history from preserved century-old railway stations to retro freight and passenger trains.

96__SOS Labyrinthe

Let's get lost

The SOS Labyrinthe in the Old Port is sandwiched between some of Montreal's most famous attractions, like La Grande Roue de Montreal and Marché Bonsecours. Despite the fact that it's perched right in the centre of the city's most beautiful neighbourhood, there's a very good chance you've walked by the entertainment venue without even noticing it.

The indoor playground is set within the walls of Hangar 16 on the Clock Tower Quay, a century-old warehouse on the banks of the Saint Lawrence River that has been used for storing cargo and merchandise since 1913. Today, it hosts SOS Labyrinthe, a sprawling network of mazes and puzzles designed to challenge families and groups of friends of all ages. According to SOS Labyrinthe's story – wink, wink – the abandoned warehouse is home to the "hidden treasures of the longshoremen," who used to work within Hangar 16. It's up to you to uncover their lost artifacts.

The mega labyrinth, at just over two kilometres (1.25 miles) in total length, is one of the largest indoor mazes in the world. It's designed to keep you guessing each time you visit, as the four hidden treasures of the longshoremen and the twists and turns along the way change monthly. So every time you visit, you'll find new and exciting challenges.

Although the SOS Labyrinthe is made for fun and thrills, it also leans into the history of the Old Port and the city's maritime heritage. Each of the "four treasures of the longshoremen" will teach you more about the neighborhood and the Hangar 16 warehouse itself.

The labyrinth is appropriate for participants of all ages, but adults looking for an extra challenge should come for "Blackout Thursdays," a special, once-a-week, after-hours, night-time event when the maze is plunged into darkness. You'll have to navigate the myriad of dead ends and traps with only a flashlight and a lot of good luck.

Address 360 Rue de la Commune E, Montreal, QC H2Y 0B4, +1 (514) 499-0099, www.soslabyrinthe.com | Getting there Metro 2 to Champ-de-Mars (Orange Line) | Hours See website for schedule | Tip Also in the Old Port you'll find A/Maze (480 Rue Saint-Jean, www.amazemontreal.com); the carefully scripted escape room experience is designed to immerse and challenge participants of all ages – from young children to adults.

97 Spa Saint James
The distinctly Quebecois maple syrup massage

You've probably heard of and maybe even enjoyed a clay, mud, or seaweed-based massage. You may have even heard about the bunches of oak leaves used during traditional Russian *venik* massages. But how about something a little sweeter for your skin, like, say, maple syrup?

Maple syrup and all its byproducts are arguably Quebec's most widely recognized export. Quebec maple syrup is available for purchase in grocery stores and specialty boutiques around the world. Apparently, the naturally sticky, sweet substance has many more uses and proven benefits outside of the kitchen as well.

The serene and spacious Spa Saint James at the Ritz-Carlton Montreal Hotel is the only wellness retreat in the city to offer a relaxation treatment that is distinctly Quebecois. Owner Jordan Saint James and his partners created the luxury hotel's Montreal signature "Maple Sugar Treatment" as a nod to Quebec's heritage and a particularly decadent way to elevate the beloved natural resource.

The exclusive treatment uses a blend of Quebec-made maple and organic vegetable oils designed to be applied in tandem with a hot stone massage, during a scalp or foot massage, or on its own as a sumptuous exfoliant during manicure and pedicure treatments. Interestingly enough, maple is packed with antioxidants, nutrients, and minerals, and as such, using maple sugar as an exfoliate or moisturizer actually helps to reduce inflammation and lighten unwanted blemishes, and it may even help to protect the skin's elasticity and slow the signs of aging. It also happens to smell really, really good.

To increase the luxury factor of your Quebecois wellness experience even more, be sure to ask your massage therapist for a cup of the hotel's exclusive Canadian maple tisane, which is included in the price of the treatment.

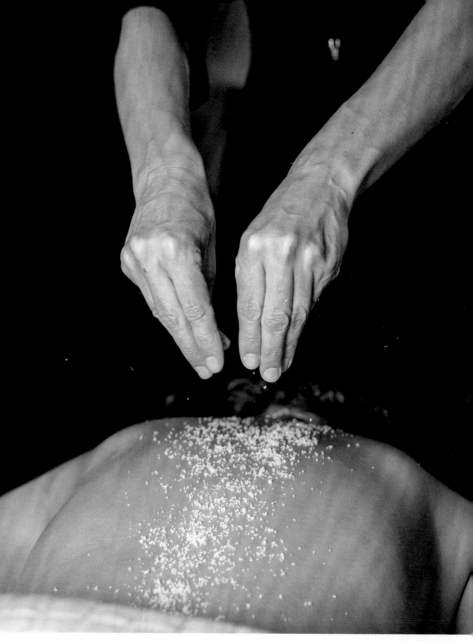

Address 1228 Rue Sherbrooke W, Montreal, QC H3G 1H6, +1 (514) 844-4590,
www,spastjames.com, info@spastjames.com | Getting there Metro 1 to Peel (Green Line) |
Hours Daily 10am–6pm | Tip Afternoon tea is served upstairs in the glamorous Palm
Court (1228 Rue Sherbrooke W, www.ritzcarlton.com/en/hotels/canada/Montreal/dining/
palm-court). The enduring tradition dates back to 1912 and gives guests an intimate look
into Montreal society a century ago.

98 Square Saint-Louis

A neighbourhood affair

Named the "closest thing to a European neighbourhood square you'll find this side of the Atlantic" by New York-based Project for Public Spaces, Square Saint-Louis between Rue Saint Denis and Avenue Laval in the Plateau is one of those laid-back and family-friendly outdoor spaces in the city that has much more historical relevance than meets the eye. The urban square doesn't get the hype of neighbouring Mont Royal or Parc La Fontaine.

Square Saint-Louis sits directly on top of the site of the city's former underground water reservoir, which was in use until the mid-1800s. It would eventually be replaced by the McTavish Reservoir closer to downtown following the Great Fire of 1852 that ravaged the city when the water source at Square Saint-Louis had been drained and closed for repairs.

By 1876, the abandoned plot of land was transformed into a public square and named for Montreal brothers and businessmen Emmanuel and Jean-Baptiste Saint-Louis. Today, the square and green space have only become more interwoven into the landscape of the Plateau neighbourhood. Square Saint-Louis serves as a multi-faceted and welcoming space, thanks to its abundance of public outdoor art and one of the first public fountains in the city, as well as the recent addition of Le K, an indoor/outdoor café stationed in a former *vespasienne*, or public urinal, at the west end of the square.

Be sure to stroll by the colourful Victorian-style houses that run along the sides of the park, as they are the true main characters of the square. The rainbow-hued residences comprise one of the largest concentrations of this style of uniquely Montreal architecture and have served as the backdrop for films, including the classic *Wait Until Dark* (1967). This square is the perfect spot to grab a latte, enjoy the historic buildings, and take in a small slice of everyday life in the city.

Address 312 Rue du Square-Saint-Louis, Montreal, QC H2X 1A5 | Getting there Metro 2 to Sherbrooke (Orange Line); bus 244 to Sherbrooke | Hours Daily 6am–midnight | Tip Randolph Pub Ludique Quartier Latin (2041 Rue Saint Denis, www.randolph.ca/en/gaming-pub/quartier-latin) is a cozy pub nearby with an expansive collection of board games and game masters available to guide you through the rules and tips for all kinds of card and board games.

99 — Squirrelgoyles
Lovable little pests at the Mount Royal Chalet

It's easy to overlook the Mount Royal Chalet, as it sits juxtaposed against one of the best views of the city. But mere metres away from the Kondiaronk Belvedere at the top of Mount Royal is a charming, little refuge designed to make spending the day exploring the trails and views of the mountain much easier and more accessible.

The chalet was built at the request of the four-time mayor of Montreal Camillien Houde (1889–1958) in 1932 as a make-work project during the Great Depression. The relatively humble, one-storey structure was conceptualized and spearheaded by Montreal architect Aristide Beaugrand-Champagne (1876–1950), who designed the chalet in a French Beaux-Arts style and took full advantage of the stunning views of Montreal below with massive, arch-top, bay windows and a regal, bricked courtyard.

Houde's vision continues to serve modern-day Montrealers and visitors attempting to climb to the peak of Mount Royal. These days, the Mount Royal Chalet functions as a café, souvenir shop, bathroom pit-stop in the summer months, and a refuge from the cold in the winter. But stepping into this cathedral-like interior is nothing like popping into a utilitarian coffee shop. In fact, it's far from it. The vast, cavernous interior design features stunning, vaulted ceilings outfitted with sophisticated chandeliers, works of art by Montreal artists, and, if you look closely, a collection of thirty-two wooden squirrel statues nestled among the exposed beams of the ceiling.

The curious "squirrelgoyles" gaze down upon visitors, each one of them nibbling on a nut while observing the goings-on below. The wooden squirrels have watched over the chalet since its inception, but it's still unclear as to who or where they came from. A nearby panel notes that they were possibly the work of the Montreal artist Elzéar Soucy (1876–1970), but their mystery remains unsolved.

Address 1196 Voie Camillien-Houde, Montreal, QC H3H 1A1, +1 (514) 843-8240, www.ville.montreal.qc.ca/siteofficieldumontroyal/batiment-municipal/chalet-mont-royal | Getting there Metro 1 to Peel (Green Line), then follow the paths to the Mount Royal Chalet about 20 minutes | Hours Daily 10am–6pm | Tip Keep weaving your way through Mount Royal Park to the Mount Royal Cross (Olmsted Trail, www.ville.montreal.qc.ca/siteofficieldumontroyal/patrimoine-artistique-commemoratif/croix-mont-royal), the imposing, steel cross given to the city in 1929 by the Société Saint-Jean-Baptiste, which stands an impressive 31 metres (102 feet) in height.

100 St. Joseph's Oratory
The beating heart of Mount Royal

The St. Joseph's Oratory in Côte-des-Neiges is one of the most frequented places of worship in the city, and not just by the Roman Catholic community. The storied oratory draws in hundreds of thousands of visitors of all faiths and creeds each year for its impressive Renaissance-revival exterior and art deco interior, something that was considered out-of-the-box in the early 20th century when the oratory was constructed.

André Bessette, more commonly known as Brother André or the Miracle Man of Montreal, became known for his reported abilities to heal those who brought their problems or illnesses to him, as if he could perform miracles. He reportedly healed hundreds of thousands of Montrealers through prayer before his death at the age of 91, when half a million people filed past his bier to pay their respects to the saint of the Congregation of Holy Cross.

Visitors who step into the oratory for the first time are often overcome by a sense of metaphysical awe, especially upon entering the Chapel of Ex-votos, or the Votive Chapel, where thousands of discarded canes and crutches are suspended from floor to ceiling in recognition of the healing powers of Brother André. Also known as ex-votos, these objects are offered when a prayer is fulfilled. And there is much more to discover beyond the chapel's doors.

Although Brother André passed away nearly a century ago, he continues to be celebrated as a miracle worker. His body is buried in a tomb under the St. Joseph's Oratory, but it's his heart that makes the trip to St. Joseph's Oratory all the more meaningful.

Brother André's heart – and some would say his ability to grant miracles – was preserved in a reliquary and remains on display within the church for the general public to pay their respects, pray for their own miracle, or simply admire the ornate reliquary and the rich theological history it represents.

Address 3800 Chemin Queen Mary, Montreal, QC H3V 1H6, +1 (514) 733-8211, www.saint-joseph.org, info@osj.qc.ca | Getting there Bus 165 or 166 to Côte-des-Neiges/ Queen-Mary | Hours Daily 6:30am–9pm, see website for tours, concerts, and events | Tip Step into the neighbouring Pavillon Jean XXIII (4725 Rue Kingston, Côte-Des-Neiges), where you'll find a quiet boutique hotel with a café and direct access to the Garden of the Way of the Cross and its impressive sculpture collection.

101 Surf the Saint Lawrence with KSF

Hang ten on Habs territory

Montreal might be 400 kilometres (250 miles) away from the Atlantic coastline, but that hasn't prevented a small yet mighty community of surfers from seeking out a decent spot to catch some waves. In fact, the Habitat 67 standing wave, named for its proximity to architect Moshe Safdie's Habitat 67 housing complex, hits nearly two metres (6.5 feet) in height and has even given way to Montreal-based river-surfing schools further down the Saint Lawrence.

River surfing is entirely different from traditional ocean surfing in that you don't have to wait for the best waves or hit the shoreline. You'll still need decent balance, strength, and patience to get into the flow of the water, but river surfing allows you to catch just one ribbon of water and ride it as long or as far as you can. Thanks to the long and gentle style of the wave, this slight shift in technique makes it much easier for amateur and beginner surfers to ride a wave without the need to keep paddling back out into the water.

You could jump with your board right into the Saint Lawrence River in the Old Port and learn as you go, but it's going to be a whole lot easier – and safer – to take a few lessons at river surfing school KSF. The LaSalle-based school, open since 1995, is located in a wider stretch of the Saint Lawrence next to the Vague à Guy, or Guy's Wave, a U-shaped rock formation near the shoreline that provides a particularly strong wave that's ripe for surfers and kayakers with advanced skills.

KSF's most popular class for beginners is the "Bunny Wave," a three-hour, comprehensive introduction to river surfing that aims to help students learn the basic techniques and necessary skills in order to build enough confidence on the water to attempt Vague à Guy and eventually surf the waves of the Old Port.

Address 7770 Boulevard LaSalle, LaSalle, QC H8P 1X6 +1 (514) 595-7873, www.ksf.ca |
Getting there Bus 58 to Bishop-Power/No 220 | Hours See website for seasonal hours
and class schedule | Tip People of all faiths are welcome inside the Gurdwara Guru Nanak
Darbar LaSalle (7801 Rue Cordner, Lasalle, www.montrealgurudwara.com), or you can
simply admire the opulent, golden-capped, Sikh place of worship and the Nishan Sahib flag
that flies 52 metres (172 feet) high.

102 T&T Supermarket

The biggest Asian supermarket in Canada

In the mood for housemade pineapple buns? Fresh durian or Japanese-inspired alpine strawberries? Maybe you're looking to stock up on Korean face masks, or you just want to grab a quick *bánh mì* and a Pocari Sweat sports drink to go. T&T Supermarket in Saint-Laurent has all your bases covered – and then some. The sprawling mega-mart is the first T&T in Quebec, and it is also considered the largest Asian supermarket in Canada.

However, the T&T origin story is admittedly much humbler. T&T's founder Cindy Lee opened her first location in 1993 in Vancouver, BC. The Taiwanese Canadian working mother of three dreamed of being able to provide families in her neighbourhood with fresh Asian food and groceries at a time when Asian products were not readily available in most markets.

T&T, named after Lee's daughters Tina and Tiffany, was a hit when it first opened over thirty years ago, rapidly expanding and eventually expanding to Montreal, where it serves both the Saint-Laurent neighbourhood and Greater Montreal, thanks to its incredible selection of over 20,000 products from different parts of Asia.

The sprawling 70,000 square-foot supermarket opens up onto a premium fruit and seasonal gifting department before bringing you into a massive produce and skincare section. Head to the back of the market, and you'll find a fresh sushi bar, barbeque station, a variety of housemade pastries and sandwiches, as well as a huge selection of imported Asian wine and beer. In true Quebec fashion, T&T's Montreal location is the only store in Canada to sell alcoholic beverages.

T&T calls itself a "grocerant" because, along with its selection of freshly made foods, the store has an ample dining room area beyond the checkout lines. After all, is there anything better than rewarding yourself with a hot snack and an iced cold drink once you've gotten your grocery shopping out of the way?

Address 300 Avenue Sainte-Croix, Montreal, QC H4N 3K4, +1 (514) 747-1240, www.tntsupermarket.com/eng | Getting there Metro 2 to Du Collège (Orange Line); bus 16, 124, 368 to Sainte-Croix/Dion | Hours Daily 8am–9pm | Tip The Musée des métiers d'art du Québec down the street (615 Avenue Sainte Croix, www.mumaq.com/en) is an artisanal museum showcasing the history of Quebec crafts in a beautiful, reclaimed, neo-Gothic church complete with confessionals and stained-glass windows.

103 The Three Bares Fountain
A comedy of errors at the McGill University campus

We often think of "white elephant" gifts as the cheeky novelty items that friends exchange over holiday dinner parties. But *The Three Graces,* more commonly called "The Three Bares," outside of McGill University took the idea to a whole new level when it arrived on campus nearly a century ago.

Gertrude Vanderbilt Whitney (1875–1942) was an American sculptor, a prominent patron of the arts, and founder of the Whitney Museum of American Art in New York City. So when she offered the university a piece of her own art that she described as "symbolic of the nation's strength implanted in the fertility of the soil" as a sign of the friendship between the United States and Canada, McGill's principal Sir Arthur Currie (1875–1933) assumed she would be sending a high-brow sculpture worthy of prominent placement.

Unfortunately for Sir Arthur, high-brow art it was not. The fountain depicts three fully nude young men in great detail, which at the time was considered to be highly offensive. The unveiling of "The Three Bares" was met with laughter and confusion, causing an uproar among more conservative faculty and critics – and it didn't stop there.

The fountain turned out to be a burden on the university's already tight, Depression-era budget. It cost a fortune in import duties and took over three years to connect the plumbing. By the time the fountain actually functioned as expected, it had developed unsightly rust stains, resulting in even more criticism from the art world and the faculty alike.

The fountain still stands prominently on the downtown campus with nary a plaque nor historical marker to acknowledge the artist or the intended symbolism. Nonetheless, "The Three Bares" remains an integral part of the McGill landscape, a resting spot for students scurrying between classes, and the most obvious place for frosh week pranks and souvenir photos on graduation day.

Address McGill University, 845 Rue Sherbrooke W, Montreal, QC H3A 0G4, +1 (514) 398-4455, www.mcgill.ca | Getting there Bus 24 to Université McGill | Hours Unrestricted | Tip Pay a visit to Place Jean-Paul-Riopelle (1000 Place Jean-Paul-Riopelle) if you want to see the splendour of a well-thought-out fountain in the city. This stunning water feature, known as La Joute, transforms into a show of fire and mist each night during the summer months.

104 Twilight Sculpture Garden

One person's trash...

"Transforming this space from what it once was – a flat and barren space littered with garbage and refuse – into a public space that is used by many as a meeting place, a picnic ground or just a place for repose has been a great pleasure to me," writes artist Glen LeMesurier. The Twilight Sculpture Garden, or the *Jardin du Crépuscule*, sits upon a formerly empty lot at the corner of Avenue Van Horne and Rue St. Urban in the Mile End neighbourhood.

The local artist has been keeping tabs on the garden from his studio down the street for over two decades and installing sculptures and whimsical works on a regular basis. He credits the garden as the home of some of his more experimental artworks and a way to think outside of the box, quite literally. He takes pride in the fact that the garden is being constantly edited and re-curated to evolve and change with time. In true Montreal fashion, many of the pieces are kinetic, designed to move with the currents of the wind and reflect the season's change. This means that the garden will almost always look different whenever you visit, depending on the season or time of year.

The garden is made up almost entirely of salvaged and recycled metal, but LeMesurier's passion for public art and his inherent scrappiness is what makes the plot of land so special when you come across it. This place has essentially become an official public park, thanks to the self-taught artist's efforts and maintenance over the years. He's given life to this formerly abandoned plot of land.

Keep an eye out for pops of bright colours among the weather-worn and rusted structures, which can act as a metaphor for the rustic neighbourhood as a whole. The gentle creak in the wind and crisscrossing of moving parts and salvaged items offer another way of looking at how public art can look like with committed care and creativity.

Address 101 Avenue Van Horne, Montreal, QC H2T 2J2 | Getting there Bus 80 to Du Parc/Van Horne or Bus 161 to Van Horne/Waverly | Hours Unrestricted | Tip Nearby, you'll find Alambika (6484 Boulevard St. Laurent, www.alambika.ca), a niche glassware shop brimming with everything from Japanese knives and wine glasses to old-school absinthe fountains.

105_ Tyrolienne MTL Zipline
Come fly with me

The boardwalk and surrounding side streets at the Old Port see millions of tourists each year. The historic waterfront district is beautiful even on the rainiest or snowiest of days, thanks to the cobblestoned streets and incredibly well-preserved examples of New France architecture, much of which dates back to the 17th century. This is one of those timeless areas that both tourists and locals can enjoy visiting time and time again. Still, there's nothing wrong with experiencing the quaint charm of the Old Port from a different perspective every once in a while.

Tyrolienne MTL Zipline is the first urban zipline circuit in Canada. Thrill-seekers have the chance to see the Old Montreal skyline in a new and refreshing way: from above. The zipline course soars over the bustling Old Port and Bonsecours Island, crossing over the water 26 metres (85 feet) up in the air. The sky-high course spans a total of 366 metres (1,200 feet) and shoots you from point A to point B at about 60 kilometres (37 miles) per hour in just 45 seconds, but adrenaline junkies will tell you that it's going to feel a lot faster.

Prepare to lose yourself in this fast-moving, family-friendly joyride. Climbing up the stairs to the launch point, you'll probably feel a jolt of anticipation and a teeny bit of adrenaline. You'll receive a security briefing, and then you'll get strapped snugly into your harness with nothing but you and the Montreal skyline in your mind. You'll know you're ready to fly!

Channelling your inner superhero, you'll soar through the air with just enough time to catch your breath and take in the bird's eye view before landing. Tyrolienne MTL Zipline calls this brief journey a once-in-a-lifetime experience, but once you've felt the weightlessness and excitement while whipping from one side of the neighbourhood to the other, you're going to want to give it another go.

Address Hangar 16, 363 Rue De La Commune E, Montreal, QC H2Y 1J3, +1 (514) 947-5463, www.mtlzipline.com, info@mtlzipline.com | **Getting there** Metro 2 to Champ-de-Mars (Orange Line); bus 14, 715 to De La Commune/De Bonsecours | **Hours** See website for seasonal schedule | **Tip** Built to celebrate the city's 375th anniversary, La Grande Roue de Montréal changed the skyline for the better. It's the tallest Ferris wheel in all of Canada and offers breath-taking views of the Old Port and Saint Lawrence River (362 Rue de la Commune E, www.lagranderouedemontreal.com).

106_ Verdun Beach
A day at the beach – in the city

Yes – you can go to the beach in Montreal! Verdun Beach might not be as big or as beautiful as those along the coastal shores of the country, but this neighbourhood park is perfect for cooling off on a hot day or basking in the sun with a bucket of cold beers.

This unique, manufactured beach is set on the banks of the Saint Lawrence River, which sounds like you might be faced with intense or advanced-level swimming conditions. But it's pretty much the opposite in reality, thanks in part to the sheltered waters sandwiched between the Island of Montreal and neighbouring Nun's Island. The swimming area and coastline are designed to be as calm as possible, with a rock dyke and a sand-filled zone, which are surrounded by rockfill to help create smooth, tranquil waterways. You can also borrow a life jacket for free if you have any lingering concerns.

The beach's convenient positioning between the two islands is made even more inclusive and family-friendly with its universal accessibility that includes a concrete path snaking its way down to the swimming area with ramp access, and loads of kid-focused activities, like slides, sandy areas dedicated to play, a gentle rock-climbing wall, and even public hammocks available for those who just want to hang out and enjoy the sights and sounds of the urban beach.

Tucked just behind the Verdun Auditorium at the corner of Rue De l'Église and Boulevard Lasalle, Verdun Beach is accessible directly from the waterfront bike path. Nearby public transit makes this a convenient destination for families and city dwellers who might not have the means to get to some of the more distant beaches outside of Montreal. And don't let its central location fool you, because once you have sand in between your toes and a view of the water, the coastline of the Saint Lawrence feels as though you're miles away from the bustling city.

Address 4110 Boulevard LaSalle, Verdun, QC H4G 2A5, +1 (514) 280-0789, https://montreal.ca/en/places/verdun-beach | Getting there Metro 1 to De l'Église (Green Line) | Hours See website for lifeguard hours | Tip Down the street is another Verdun Beach (4816 Rue Wellington, www.barverdunbeach.com), but this one is a quirky wine and cocktail bar named after the neighbouring waterfront park.

107 __ Westmount Lawn Bowling & Croquet Club

A social club on the green grass

Walking on Sherbrooke between Clarke and Kensington is always a breath of fresh air from the edge of Westmount and bustling downtown. In true Westmount fashion, the three-block stretch of green space is almost always lush and vibrant, and mature trees and foliage dot the sidewalk along the way. This stretch is particularly good for strolling and people-watching.

But have you ever stopped to take a peek over the hedge-lined clubhouse at the corner of the street? If you have, you've probably wondered what the dozens of colourful balls spread out on the green space and the dozens of people mulling about the lawn clad in all white are doing there. The Westmount Lawn Bowling & Croquet Club has called this address home for over a century, first opening in the spring of 1902 and has continued to serve as one of the few lawn bowling and croquet venues in the city ever since.

The club was first proposed by James Brown, James Baillie, and James Rodgers, three immigrants from Scotland. Together, they wrote an open letter to the Westmount inhabitants, advertising the potential development of a bowling green. The idea became a reality when the clubhouse was built for less than $500 in under a year. It quickly accumulated more than a hundred members by 1903. These days, the charming, olive-hued clubhouse has been revamped and modernized to include a modern kitchen and communal sitting area to better serve members and onlookers, but it retains the century-old charm that the three Scots had envisioned.

Note that the Westmount Lawn Bowling Club is still members-only. Anyone can apply for a variety of annual membership options, but if you're not sure about whether the game is for you, fear not. Regular tournaments take place on the front lawn.

Address 401 Avenue Kensington, Westmount, QC H3Y 3A2, +1 (514) 989-5532, www.bowlswestmount.ca, info@bowlswestmount.ca | Getting there Bus 24, 104, 138, 456 to Sherbrooke O/Redfern | Hours See website for bowling schedule | Tip Part bowling alley, part LGBTQIA+ bar, part pizza parlour, Bar Notre-Dame-Des-Quilles (32 Rue Beaubien E, www.facebook.com/notredamedesquilles) is a unique and delicious spot to let loose and test your hand at traditional pin bowling.

108_ Westmount Public Library

Check out the postcard collection

The Westmount Public Library is the oldest municipal *bibliothèque* in the province. Dating back to 1897, the establishment still provides the Westmount neighbourhood with ample books and reference material to discover within the confines of the red-bricked, Tudor Revival building. The picturesque community space is recessed into Westmount Park and flanked by its own public conservatory and greenhouse complete with tropical plants and soaring glass ceilings. Can you imagine a better spot to stop and smell the roses with your library book in hand?

The public library and reading room was built in commemoration of Queen Victoria's Diamond Jubilee under the condition that it "shall be forever free to the use of the inhabitants and ratepayers of the town." It has borne witness to the expansion and urbanisation of Montreal and still operates under these conditions. The library stands out for its commitment to family-friendly activities and keeping the community engaged in reading and acquiring knowledge. And it stays true to its past and the roots of the Westmount neighbourhood within Greater Montreal with a special collection.

Established in 1974 to commemorate the library's 75th anniversary, the Postcard Collection offers a unique visual history of Quebec that goes back to the 1890s. The special collection consists of over 13,000 personalized postcards by way of donations that had been arriving at the library for over 50 years, adding to the history of Westmounters and Montrealers through unique personal narratives.

The precious collection of hand-written postcards is under lock and key within the library collections, but you can see these originals by appointment. If you're dropping by the library and want to get an idea of the vastness of the collection without an appointment, photocopies of the postcards are available at the reference desk upon request.

Address 4574 Rue Sherbrooke O, Westmount, QC H3Z 1G1, +1 (514) 989-5300,
www.westlib.org | Getting there Bus 24 to Sherbrooke/Strathcona | Hours Mon–Fri
10am–9pm, Sat & Sun 10am–5pm | Tip The Victoria Hall Community Centre (4626 Rue
Sherbrooke O, westmount.org/en/victoria-hall-community-centre) is a stunning neo-Tudor
style facility with a community-led art gallery featuring local Westmount artists.

109_ The Wheel Club

Hillbilly Night in the middle of the metropolis

Montreal might be internationally renowned for its indie music halls and cosmopolitan concert venues, but residents of Notre-Dame-de-Grâce know that one of the best spots to take in a music performance in the city is in a subterranean address just off Rue Sherbrooke.

The original Wheel Club began as a veterans' social club, and over the years it transformed into a diverse arts and culture hub for musicians, with a major emphasis on bluegrass and country music. The only performance venue of its kind in Montreal draws crowds of all ages and walks of life, thanks partly to its engaged team of artists, creatives, and volunteers that have kept its open mic tradition alive, while fostering a sense of community and promoting greater accessibility to performance art and live music.

Considered to be the longest-running open mic night in Montreal, the Wheel Club and its infamous "Hillbilly Night" have championed budding and veteran bluegrass and country musicians since its inception over fifty years ago. The Wheel Club's director, professional musician and Cirque du Soleil alumnus Clifford Schwartz, aims to preserve the old-time country music club through community engagement and a handful of strict rules: no drums, amplifiers, or electric instruments, and absolutely no songs that post-date 1969.

The renowned "Hillbilly Night" takes place every Monday night without fail. Even during the COVID-19 pandemic, the Wheel Club took open mic nights online and accessible to anyone with a Wi-Fi connection. The happening has earned a reputation for its inclusive atmosphere, as many different generations and walks of life come together to sing the blues, appreciate the banjo and bass, and let loose in a safe and fun atmosphere. Admission is free for all who are interested in checking out the country music club experience. Dancing and singing along are highly encouraged!

Address 3373 Boulevard Cavendish, Montreal, QC H4B 2L7, +1 (514) 489-3322, www.wheelclubndg.com, info@wheelclubndg.com | Getting there Bus 105, 356, 420 to Cavendish/Sherbrooke O | Hours See website for showtimes | Tip Prefer jazz to bluegrass? Head west to the Upstairs Jazz Bar & Grill (1254 Rue Mackay, www.upstairsjazz.com), another subterranean music venue hosting some of the country's top jazz musicians on a nightly basis.

110 Wilensky's Light Lunch
The rules are the rules

When ordering a Special, you should know a thing or two. It is always served with mustard; it is never cut for you. Don't ask us why; just understand that this is nothing new. This is the way that it's been done since 1932.

The sing-song claim plastered on the wall at Wilensky's Light Lunch seems lighthearted, but you really do need to follow the guidelines to the letter if you want to patronize this Mile End sandwich and soda shop. The family-run institution claims that when a business has been around for such a long time, it may require its own set of rules. Don't worry, though, as long as you don't ask for mods – especially on your Wilensky Special, a grilled, all-beef salami and all-beef baloney sandwich with just a hint of mustard – or try to insist on leaving a tip, you'll be just fine.

The neighbourhood restaurant will make you feel like you've stepped nearly 100 years back in time. In case you hadn't noticed, Wilensky's is a stickler for tradition, and the small dining space has retained much of the original charm that made it such a hit back in the 1930s. The old-fashioned soda machine still serves up homemade drinks. The decades-old grill continues to cook Wilensky Specials to perfection. The pressed tin ceiling and wood-panelled, turquoise walls adorned with retro décor and memorabilia add to the veritable time machine that is the Wilensky dining space.

The Wilensky family's history of serving the Mile End neighbourhood runs deeper than just the legacy sandwich shop. Harry Wilensky emigrated from Russia to Montreal in the late 1800s, where he started his family and a whole lot of business ventures. His barbershop, cigar shop, and variety store eventually gave way to a book stand and soda shop which, years later, opened the doors to the addition of a grill, where son Moe Wilensky invented the famed, present-day Wilensky Special.

Address 34 Avenue Fairmount W, Montreal, QC H2T 2M1, +1 (514) 271-0247, www.top2000.ca/wilenskys, info@wilenskys.com | Getting there Bus 55, 363 to Saint-Laurent/Fairmount | Hours Tue–Sat 10am–4pm | Tip Around the corner is Parc Lahaie (4921 Boulevard Saint-Laurent) a well-appointed public square complete with a ton of benches and a stunning central fountain set against the Saint-Enfant-Jésus Catholic church.

111_Windsor Station
The former hub for Canadian travel

If you wanted to travel east to Nova Scotia or westward to Alberta and British Columbia a century ago, you wouldn't be dragging your dinged-up suitcase to Dorval. Instead, you'd be elegantly dressed and making your way to Windsor Station, the hub of Canadian travel during the railway boom. The building functioned as the city's Canadian Pacific Railway (CPR) station from 1889 to 1996, serving thousands of travellers heading east and west. It was named as a Heritage Railway Station in 1990, and it represents the major role Montreal played in the early days of Canadian coast-to-coast travel.

Despite its former glory and significance in the domestic travel space, Windsor Station no longer serves commuters. To catch a train out of town, you'll have to walk a few blocks over to the decidedly less glamourous Gare Centrale. However, this National Historic Site has been carefully preserved for railway buffs to experience the magnificence of 19th-century train travel.

The stunning, Romanesque Revival-style building was erected during a time when railway companies were constantly competing and trying to one-up each other, which meant no detail was spared. Windsor Station was built by American architect Bruce Price (1845–1903), the very same man behind other iconic Canadian buildings, including the Château Frontenac in Quebec City. Once inside this magnificent, ornate station, you'll marvel at its stunning archways, vaulted ceilings, and gables.

The carefully preserved, former railway concourse, known as the *Salle des pas perdus*, still hosts the original "Arrivals and Departures" boards that harken back to the splendour of railway travel. You'll also want to make your way to the far end of the lobby to appreciate the moving *Angel of Victory* monument by Coeur de Lion McCarthy (1881–1979) in remembrance of the CPR employees who perished in World War I.

Address 1100 Avenue des Canadiens-de-Montréal, Montreal, QC H3C 2H8 | Getting there Metro 2 to Bonaventure (Orange Line); bus 75, 107, 420, 715 to Peel/Saint-Antoine | Hours Unrestricted | Tip Visit the Hyatt Centric (621 Rue Notre-Dame E, www.hyatt.com/hyatt-centric/yulct-hyatt-centric-ville-marie-montreal) in the Old Port for a glass of wine or espresso. The old-meets-new hotel is set within a 125-year-old, former railway hotel and right next to Place Gare Viger, one of the oldest train stations in Canada.

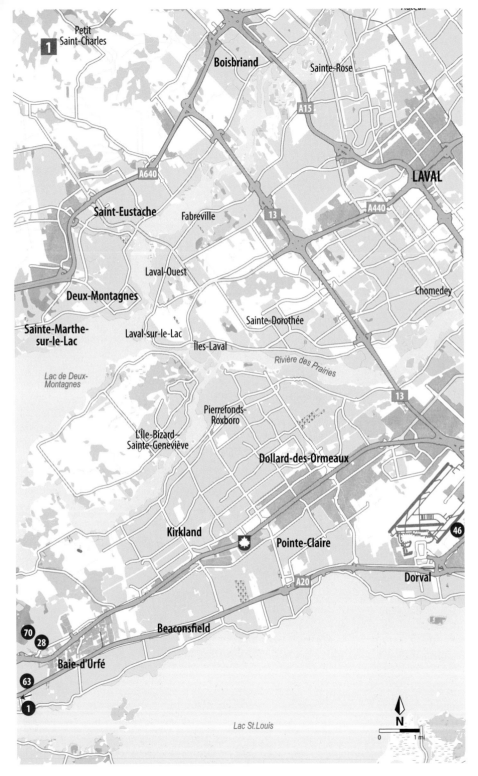

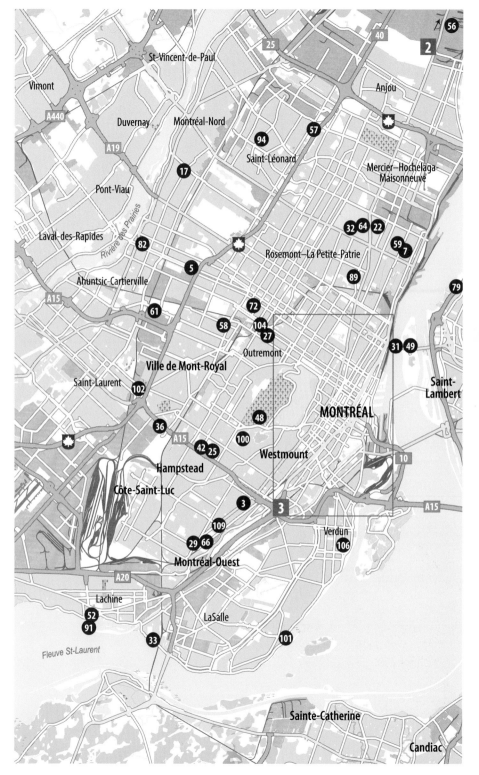

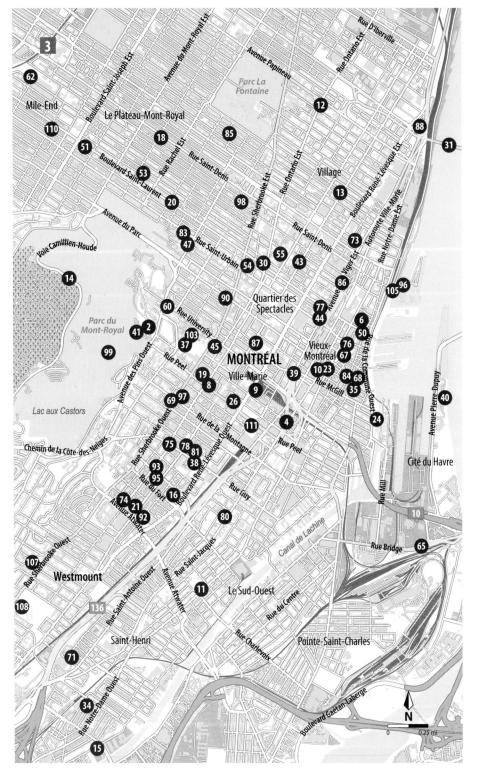

Dave Doroghy, Graeme Menzies
111 Places in Victoria
That You Must Not Miss
ISBN 978-3-7408-1720-6

Dave Doroghy, Graeme Menzies
111 Places in Vancouver
That You Must Not Miss
ISBN 978-3-7408-2150-0

Dave Doroghy, Graeme Menzies
111 Places in Whistler
That You Must Not Miss
ISBN 978-3-7408-1046-7

Jennifer Bain, Liz Beddall
111 Places in Ottawa
That You Must Not Miss
ISBN 978-3-7408-1388-8

Jennifer Bain, Christina Ryan
111 Places in Calgary
That You Must Not Miss
ISBN 978-3-7408-0749-8

Elizabeth Lenell-Davies,
Anita Genua, Claire Davenport
111 Places in Toronto
That You Must Not Miss
ISBN 978-3-7408-0257-8

Jo-Anne Elikann, Susan Lusk
111 Places in New York
That You Must Not Miss
ISBN 978-3-7408-1888-3

Wendy Lubovich, Ed Lefkowicz
111 Museums in New York
That You Must Not Miss
ISBN 978-3-7408-0379-7

Wendy Lubovich, Jean Hodgens
111 Places in the Hamptons
That You Must Not Miss
ISBN 978-3-7408-1891-3

Brian Hayden, Jesse Pitzler
111 Places in Buffalo
That You Must Not Miss
ISBN 978-3-7408-2151-7

Kim Windyka, Heather Kapplow,
Alyssa Wood
111 Places in Boston
That You Must Not Miss
ISBN 978-3-7408-1558-5

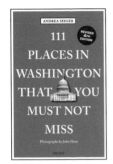

Andréa Seiger, John Dean
111 Places in Washington
That You Must Not Miss
ISBN 978-3-7408-1890-6

Brandon Schultz, Lucy Baber
111 Places in Philadelphia
That You Must Not Miss
ISBN 978-3-7408-1376-5

Allison Robicelli, John Dean
111 Places in Baltimore
That You Must Not Miss
ISBN 978-3-7408-1696-4

Amy Bizzarri, Susie Inverso
111 Places in Chicago
That You Must Not Miss
ISBN 978-3-7408-1030-6

Michelle Madden, Janet McMillan
111 Places in Milwaukee
That You Must Not Miss
ISBN 978-3-7408-1643-8

Sandra Gurvis, Mitch Geiser
111 Places in Columbus
That You Must Not Miss
ISBN 978-3-7408-0600-2

Harriet Baskas, Cortney Kelley
111 Places in Seattle
That You Must Not Miss
ISBN 978-3-7408-1992-7

Katrina Nattress, Jason Quigley
**111 Places in Portland
That You Must Not Miss**
ISBN 978-3-7408-0750-4

Floriana Petersen, Steve Werney
**111 Places in San Francisco
That You Must Not Miss**
ISBN 978-3-7408-1698-8

Floriana Petersen, Steve Werney
**111 Places in Silicon Valley
That You Must Not Miss**
ISBN 978-3-7408-1346-8

Laurel Moglen, Julia Posey,
Lyudmila Zotova
**111 Places in Los Angeles
That You Must Not Miss**
ISBN 978-3-7408-1889-0

Brian Joseph
**111 Places in Hollywood
That You Must Not Miss**
ISBN 978-3-7408-1819-7

Kelsey Roslin, Nic Yeager,
Jesse Pitzler
**111 Places in Austin
That You Must Not Miss**
ISBN 978-3-7408-1642-1

Dana DuTerroil, Joni Fincham,
Daniel Jackson
**111 Places in Houston
That You Must Not Miss**
ISBN 978-3-7408-1697-1

Dana DuTerroil, Joni Fincham,
Sara S. Murphy
**111 Places for Kids in Houston
That You Must Not Miss**
ISBN 978-3-7408-1372-7

Philip D. Armour, Susie Inverso
**111 Places in Denver
That You Must Not Miss**
ISBN 978-3-7408-1220-1

A huge thank you to my friends and family who listened to me wax on and on about the wonderful little intricacies of Montreal for the past two years while I was writing this book – and especially to those who tagged along while I was scouting locations across the city.

I want to thank my mom in particular for encouraging me to follow my dreams wherever they take me. I always knew I would write a book, and her unwavering belief in me and encouragement since I first brought up writing at age four has been a driving force from the start.

Thank you to my dad, my brothers, my stepparents, and to my irreplaceable grandmothers, who never said no to taking me to the library growing up (even if it was every day) and who encouraged me to leave my comfy nest in Nova Scotia for a new adventure in Montreal all those years ago. I'm grateful to have had such strong and independent women by my side to cheer me on.

I also want to thank my wonderful editor Karen for putting up with my puppy-like enthusiasm for this project and for making the book what it is, and to Bethany for bringing the visual aspect to life so beautifully.

And *merci mille fois* to the city of Montreal. There's no place in the world I would have rather spent my twenties. You rock. Don't ever change.

Kaitlyn McInnis

Harry – Words can't express my gratitude to you. Through snowstorms, ice storms early mornings and lots and lots of driving you were there through it all. Your support and encouragement has meant more than you know, and this wouldn't have been possible without you.

To my dear friends in Montreal, the three of you have been by my side and supported me through this photo journey. Your generosity has been a true blessing, and I am deeply grateful for your kindness. Thank you from the bottom of my heart.

To Karen and the Emons team, thank you for the opportunity to undertake this project. I have learned and grown so much from this experience! Kaitlyn, you wrote beautifully about a fabulous city. I know people will love learning the stories within these pages.

Bethany Livingstone

Kaitlyn McInnis is a Montreal-based travel writer committed to helping you plan your next holiday. Her work has been featured in international publications across six continents, including *Condé Nast Traveler*, *Travel + Leisure*, *South China Morning Post*, *CNN.com*, *Tatler*, and more. She holds a Bachelor of Arts focused in English Literature and Irish Studies from Concordia University and a Master of Fine Arts in Creative Nonfiction from the University of King's College in Nova Scotia.

Bethany Livingstone is a photographer originally from Prince Edward Island. She developed a passion for travel photography from traveling across five continents. She's currently living in Ottawa and specializing in political portraits and lifestyle photography. She has strong personal connections in Montreal and a great affection for the city. Her work has been featured in online publications and in private collections across North America. www.marleyimaging.com